EBRAHIM HUSSEIN:
Swahili Theatre and Individualism

EBRAHIM HUSSEIN:
Swahili Theatre and Individualism

Alain Ricard

(translated from French by Dr. Nàomi Morgan)

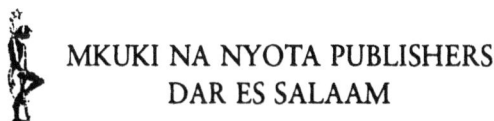

MKUKI NA NYOTA PUBLISHERS
DAR ES SALAAM

EBRAHIM HUSSEIN:
Swahili Theatre and Individualism

«Em poder e forcas muito excede A Moáambique esta ilha, que se chama Quiloa, mui conhecida pela fama...»

«For in power and in strength it greatly surpasses Mozambique, this island well known by fame, called Quiloa...»
(Camoens, Lusiads, Stanza 99)

First published in French by Karthala,
22-24, boulevard Arago - 75013, Paris

This translation is published by
Mkuki na Nyota Publishers
6 Muhonda, Mission Quarter, Kariakoo
P. O. Box 4246
Dar es Salaam
Tanzania

©Alain Ricard, 2000

ISBN 9976 973 81 0

Photograph and cover design by Petra of
Petra's Maridadi, Dar es Salaam

This publication benefited from the support of the Embassy of France in Tanzania and the French Institute for Research in Africa (IFRA) in Nairobi, Kenya

All rights reserved. No part of this publication may be reproduced, stored in a retrival system or transmitted in any form or by any means without prior written permission of Mkuki na Nyota Publishers.

Contents

Acknowledgements ix

Introduction xi

Chapter 1
A Haven of Peace 1

Chapter 2
Writing for the Theatre 13

Chapter 3
Readings: History 35

Chapter 4
Readings: Politics 55

Chapter 5
Being Swahili 70

Chapter 6
Sheikh Ebrahim: Actor and Martyr 90

Chapter 7
Between the Sea and the Walls 115

Post Script 133

Bibliography of the works of Ebrahim Hussein (1943 -) 134

Bibliography 136

Acknowledgements

This text could not have been written without the help of my friend Jean Copans who has supported my Swahili projects; without the assistance of Micheline Larrue who agreed to take into consideration that learning Kiswahili could form part of the permanent training of a researcher at the CNRS. Georges Mertens and Elena Bertoncini reread my translations, and always helped me with friendly advice. I owe thanks to Alamin Mazrui who nourished my thinking with his warm-hearted, generous intelligence. Also to Joachim Fiebach, who shared his experience as a theorist and as a friend of Ebrahim with me. Walter Bgoya took me to see Ebrahim several times, he also revised and adapted the translation from Kiswahili to English for the present edition. Birmganine Ndagano, Kasoro Tumbwe, François Constantin, Michael Gilsenan, Didier Morin, Mwatha Ngalasso and Jean-Claude Penrad facilitated my entry into the Bantu world and that of Islam. Raia Timmamy endured the mistakes of her pupil for two years and Claude and Marie Pierre Theis received the traveller. Last but not least, Jean-François Bayard thought that a literary essay had a place in his collection, thus contradicting the comments I make in the introduction.

The translation was prepared by Dr Nàomi Morgan, Dept of French, University of South Africa.

Introduction

In 1984 I obtained a passage to Zanzibar by a lucky combination of circumstances. The island was opening up to the outside world, twenty years after a violent revolution, followed by the massacre and exodus of a part of its population. The hidden face of the United Republic of Tanzania thus showed itself to me: a little, silent, corrupt police-state, crowned by a magnificent museum and the former Sultan's palace, renamed the House of Wonder and closed to visitors.

A few years later I visited the House of Wonder which they had decided to open on the occasion of an official visit.

Fidel Castro had pride of place at the top of the stairs. Karume, the first president (1964-1972) was a sort of new Sultan, and the ignominious Arab feudalism exploded from every wall. At a time when Arab investors were being solicited, such vehemence was no longer befitting. What's more, all the important events which had occurred since the end of feudalism in 1964 were still shrouded in mystery. What actually happened in 1964? How had Karume been assassinated a few years later? What had become of the controversial Okello, whose decisive role at the beginning of the revolution had not been mentioned? All this which had been 'forgotten' weighed heavily upon the consciences of the coastal inhabitants. Many must have felt solidarity with their co-religionists and communities whose historical destiny they shared. Ebrahim Hussein from Kilwa - a city which had depended on the Sultans of Zanzibar until the beginning of the century - must have thought about the clove-tree island, even if he spoke very little about it. Could the enthusiasm of many for benevolent, chaotic Tanzanian socialism make people forget about the small tropical *Gulag* which Karume's island had become?

What I knew about Tanzanian culture at that stage, more than ten years ago, clearly showed that, as in the case of many African countries, a totalising concept of culture had tried to take root. The personality cult had been challenged on the continent, but not in Zanzibar. Admittedly, the United Republic of Tanzania was not the USSR; and the *Ujamaa* villages were not internment camps. But Tanzania's socialist cultural and political unity-project was a totalising one and it left very little space for the autonomy of artistic creation - Ebrahim's space. Yet to us, this autonomy appears to be, along with religious freedom, one of the essential guarantees indicating that the totalising project did not develop into a totalitarian one. Basically, Ebrahim no longer agrees; but he is left in peace, he is not re-educated, he is not sent to a camp. In his own light-hearted way he resembles the man Claude Lefort talks about - the one who is always in the way. He has suffered no direct violence, apart from a few murky episodes which have left an indelible mark on him, which he often refers to, and which I have not been able to elucidate, apart from the Kenyan episode mentioned in Chapter 6.

The question about the autonomy of artistic creation leads to that of the autonomy of the individual. Today, Ebrahim is alone: does that make him an individualist? I don't know. His Tanzanian critics are forever reproaching him for his *ubinafsi* (individualism). Does any writing exist which is not individual? How can the subject's experience not be borne by an original trajectory? Ebrahim speaks for a generation – this can be seen in his first plays. And he writes in a language that unifies the country. Everything he writes, is a model: the writer is master of the language, not only of the style. It is also a question of lexis, or even of written form.

Ebrahim's oeuvre is contemporaneous with the development and planning of standard Swahili - *Kiswahili Sanifu*. The first unilingual standard dictionary was published in 1981. The best bilingual dictionary between the standard Swahili and a European language was published in 1987 and all of Ebrahim's words can be found in it. It is a Swahili-Russian dictionary which contains thirty thousand words - a remarkable work. I had to recall that I had studied Russian, known well a country that no longer exists, the Soviet Union. For my first research assignment I had also thought about a degree in Soviet criticism. I think that helped me to understand the direct and indirect pressures exerted on Ebrahim - the imaginary or real constraints he foresees.

The position of a linguistic model is particularly delicate for the person occupying it. The constantly scrutinised text receives an echo that is decreased by the supposedly exemplary virtues of its language. Such is the construction situation from the top of a national culture, which Olivier Roy analyses with regard to Soviet Central Asia, fairly similar to the Tanzanian case. Ebrahim tried to avoid this strange situation, to protect the singularity of his voice in this new language in which he was writing. All languages are shared and shared alike, but a language which is being adapted, as literary production develops, imposes strange constraints on the writer's work.

Writing becomes entirely socialised and reduced to the aims of society, not in pursuit of a truth which would come forth from its own movement. The voice has to be in harmony with party ideology, its official speeches and political cant. But writing is green and not dried-out. I like the image of Zanzibar's jujube tree - forever green until a creeper chokes it and turns it into dead wood. A living voice, the perpetually new rhythm of abrasive writing in search of truth, embarked upon a spiritual quest not directly inscribed in the instituted religions, but not scornful of them either. Such is Ebrahim's writing. He proceeds by allusions, images, ellipses - but always in the same direction.

Ebrahim's silent dissidence was not audible in the concert of the 'scientific' debates of the seventies, on the construction of socialism, of which Jean Copans' collection gives us a glimpse. Who pays attention to theatrical output? In his book on Tanzanian political culture, Denis Martin does not quote Ebrahim and does not deal with literature, although he analyses the theatricalisation of power. The writer is a dropout who does not take part in the political discourse, who rebels against political cant. There is enough material here for another debate, a methodological one, about the position of studies on literatures in our knowledge about societies. Why, in all the French and English writings on Tanzania, is there so little interest in literature in general, and in Ebrahim's work in particular?

I am engaging in an exercise in interpretation here. My hypotheses germinated during the daily discussions I had, for more than two years, with Kenyan students, as I will explain in Chapter 3. They are also the product of my meetings with Ebrahim, and of my trips to Tanzania, during which I found that Ebrahim's vision was (perhaps) the most lucid. Later I read, translated and had my translations checked by colleagues - Georges Mertens and Elena Bertoncini. I accept responsibility for any limitations. This slow revelation of his work modified my hypotheses, and invalidated a few of them. But the central thesis was validated: that there had been a divorce between the sixties activist, and the socialist Tanzanian regime. This break could be understood from Ebrahim's comments and his erratic behaviour, according to my Tanzanian interlocutors.

In the literary text Hussein calls out to us. In my own way, I try to practise the interpolative reading which Todorov conducts on our canonical writers. Hussein's texts interpolate us as they interpolate the pupil, the student and the Tanzanian intellectual. Tired of the lack of response, the author stops publishing at a certain point, although he continues writing. This silence is a new message, a new interpolation!

Another of my hypotheses is the internal coherence of his work and his approach. An original voice speaks to us with his words, with their flow. This voice signals a singular report to the world. For too long sociologists have locked us into strategies of symbolic investments pursued from within cultural fields. Indeed, Ebrahim has considerable cultural capital, which Tanzanian critics have been pleased to point out. He is the son of a large family from Kilwa and has become the best known Tanzanian dramatist. The religious cultural capital which his family holds was converted into a theatre show in his work. This tells us nothing of the dynamics and the movement of his work, nor of its unique link with the world.

The postulate of the work's unity is all the more difficult to maintain because there is often personality dissociation, or split personality. But coherence is the aim and the writing bears witness to a sometimes, painful effort to maintain it, in spite the threatening chaos in the last published work. The coherence postulate is also undermined by the multiplicity of types of expression. Naturalist theatre makes way for epic theatre and this is followed by a poetic monologue, announcing poetic prose in free-verse, as though a voice were looking for a rhythm, as though a subject were trying to situate its historical presence in the language. This mixture of poetic and dramatic genres, this lyrical and epic text, flavoured with literary and religious references, is confusing.

Ebrahim's dramas are written in free verse. He, in fact, invented Swahili free verse. These innovations are a new way of experiencing Swahili Creole. Instead of reifying the coastal identity, of essentialising Swahili, Ebrahim shows it at work. However, no one is grateful to him for this or even seems to understand the undertaking, which is only a continuation of the coastal world's tradition of opening up to the outside world. Persia, Arabia, Portugal, Germany, Great Britain, and even France (for a few decades, as far as Kilwa was concerned) came to these regions to meet black Africa in order to traffic in men, goods and ideas. The result is a culture which is very much alive, and of which Ebrahim is a part.

One can read Ebrahim in order to learn Kiswahili. This is what I did, and it is without doubt the best model one can find for the standard language. But by reading him one learns something else. Ebrahim has taken a road that cannot keep to the boundaries of the official speeches by which he is hemmed in. He feels that he has been entrusted with the history of an open, crossbred Africa - of modern Swahiliism that is secular and demanding as far as truth is concerned - which the *Uzawa* ideologists (born on the continent as true Africans or true Muslims) would want to deny.

The more I read, the more I became imbued with this imaginary nature of liberation. His humanist message contained nothing that could offend the Mwalimu, the schoolmaster who was also President - Julius Nyerere. But the 'sunglasses' and the 'hands full of jasmine' of Mwalimu's friends veiled the message, then let it fall into oblivion. But the poet remembers what it was.

Key to dramas referred to in the text

WU: *Wakati Ukuta*

AL: *Alikiona*

KI: *Kinjeketile*

MA: *Mashetani*

JK: *Jogoo Kijijini*

NJ: *Ngao ya Jadi*

AR: *Arusi*

KU: *Kwenye Ukingo wa Thim*

The texts of communication or articles published in reviews have been re-used in adapted form in certain chapters:

Chapter 5:   Identité et pouvoir dans l'oeuvre d'Ebrahim Hussein, in Macht der Identitat-Identitat der macht, Bayreuth, 1994, pp. 457-468.

Chapter 6:   Colloque sur le secret, motif et moteur de la littérature, Université Catholique de Louvain (1996): Ebrahim Hussein Secret pacte, devinette, trois modalites d'une parole cachee.

Chapter 7:   Ebrahim Hussein, poeta tra mare e muri, Africa e Mediteraneo, Bologna, 1996, 3, pp 35-39.

The poem Ukuta wa Berlin was published in Traversées de l'Afrique, Cahiers du Centre regional des lettres d'Aquitaine, 1997, 2.

1
A Haven of Peace

Walks with Ebrahim Hussein in Dar es Salaam - *Bandari Salama*: the haven of peace (Loire, 1993) - shaped my work and made me comprehend the way in which an author, whose voice I had only heard, sometimes with difficulty in translation, views the world. In dated *italics* I will quote extracts from the diary I kept during my September 1995 visit. They contain my reflections, as well as the remarks of the man I call Ebrahim, and the author I call Ebrahim Hussein. This distinction gradually blurs in the course of our exchanges and as my central hypothesis, that of the work's unity and coherence develops.

Our meetings followed an almost immutable protocol. After an introduction in Kiswahili, we spent the rest of the time speaking English. In 1997 Ebrahim sometimes spoke to me in French and he often reverted to German. We mostly spoke while walking, looking at the houses, the streets, or while seated in a café; never at his home, never in one of the traditional places in Kariakoo, the popular Swahili neighbourhood where he lives. Our meetings lasted a few hours and it was mostly Ebrahim who spoke. He doesn't like quoting his dramas, and doesn't refer to them often. On the other hand, he often alludes to current affairs, to Shakespeare, to Brecht and to Mwalimu Julius Nyerere.

I told him I wanted to write a book about him, but that I didn't want to record what he was saying. I hadn't brought a tape-recorder. The theatre is an ephemeral art. I didn't want to formalise our discussions; I wanted them to retain something of their wandering, improvised nature, that of an amicable exchange between colleagues, as we shared an admiration for Soyinka, for Brecht - even though my knowledge of Brecht did not match his.

Ebrahim Hussein lives right in the Swahili quarter, the name of which according to him is of French origin: "karia koo", that is "carrier corps" the "corps" of the "carriers", the porters, the auxiliaries of the indigenous scouts. A far-fetched etymology? Who knows! Ebrahim Hussein started his university career with W. Whiteley, founder of modern Swahili studies. When I visit him, he wants to go and have a drink in town. Dar es Salaam was built at the end of the last century on a site conceded to the Germans by the Sultan of Zanzibar. The Reich provided it with a station, warehouses and customs. The Catholic and Lutheran churches are at the water's edge, as is the residence of the former governor. A beach runs alongside the city, invaded by fishermen selling their catch in a permanent market. A ferry shuttles across the narrow channel. All streets lead to a roundabout, in the centre of which the *askari*, the scout who guaranteed the success of the English troops during the 1914 - 1919 war, described by William Boyd in *An Ice Cream War* (1993), has been given a place of honour.

German East Africa did not adhere to the armistice, and General Von Lettow Vorbeck pursued a solitary combat. The *askari* deserved more from the British Empire than the lightweight statue cast in his honour. No comparison with the monument erected for Cecil Rhodes in Cape Town: esteem is also measured in bronze weight.

In an equatorial town, the coast is the unhealthiest place. The colonialists planted eucalyptus and banyan trees; there were already a few baobabs, and the avenues along the shore look well kept. The African neighbourhoods have been relegated to the interior, to the marshlands along the river flowing north of the town. Between the German and European towns and the African neighbourhoods there is a big, open space. As in Zanzibar, it is called *Mnazi Mmoja*, one coconut tree, an allusion, according to Sacleux, to the cyclone on 15 April 1872 which left a single coconut palm tree standing in a neighbourhood in Zanzibar, that subsequently acquired that name.

At the time of Independence in 1961, President Nyerere erected a monument there, symbolising the flame of Independence. The new flame that would light Africa's way and which was carried all the way to the summit of Kilimanjaro, Africa's highest point at 5,985 metres.

---

[1] Ebrahim Hussein is not right on this point. Kariakoo in Dar es Salaam and in Nairobi, Kenya, does not have German or French origins. For a detailed explanation see Laura Sykes and Uma Waide, 1997, *Dar es Salaam: A Dozen Drives Around the City,* Dar es Salaam: Mkuki na Nyota Publishers, p.33. (Publishers' note).

Today Mnazi Mmoja is a green park, encircled by avenues arriving from the outlying parts of town. The area is occupied by a cultural centre and a school. It is a place one passes through, rather than a walkway or a meeting-place. Ebrahim lives 200 metres away from Mnazi Mmoja in Kariakoo, at the corner of Sikukuu and Udowe streets, next to the mosque of the *Manyema* (people from the interior, brought here by slave-trading caravans from the west of Lake Tanganyika, who aided and abetted the Arabs). In Ebrahim's street there is an enormous garage housing beautiful gleaming trucks and containers registered in San Francisco and bound for China. There is also a Zanzibari restaurant, selling octopus, which stays closed on Fridays. Opposite Ebrahim there is another restaurant, called Hawaii, which also closes on Fridays.

Between Mnazi Mmoja and the European part of town we pass through Indian markets. The Indians are not all Hindus, far from it - they are mostly Muslim. Admittedly, a Swami with an indecipherable name has his temple quite close to Ebrahim, but the Ismaili institutions start further off: school, mosques, hospitals. We know the Begum from her racing stables, but here the faithful of the Aga Khan are people who believe in material progress: they have opened a high school, along with a library. During the sixties, Dar's progressive Muslim youth, like Ebrahim, attended these institutions. Ebrahim still has great admiration for the philosophy of the Aga Khan, who has invested so much in his country's culture.

The fringe of the European quarter harbours many streets with Indian names. For example, Gandhi Street. I don't know India, but I imagine that these tall, five to six storey houses, geometric, with large glass surfaces typical of the fifties, resemble the modern buildings of Bombay. The latter also boasts Ismaili mosques. Even closer to the harbour there is an enormous mosque, criss-crossed with minarets with the strange, onion-shaped domes of the duodecimal Shiites, of the faith of Imam Khomeini. We often pass these believers in the Indian quarter, a mixture of Hindus and Shiites of different persuasions. Mosque Street, written in French, harbours a Sunni mosque: undoubtedly Comorans. There are many shops. The more discreet Ibadite mosques don't sparkle: the walls are plastered with white roughcast, and the minaret does not emerge from the roofs. The shopkeepers are often on their doorsteps, negotiating with workmen or cart-pushers. Business seems to be booming - the shop windows are full of imported wares.

To go downtown from where Ebrahim lives, to the harbour where bars and restaurants have opened, is to pass through a diverse part of the world: going from Islam to Hinduism and to Christianity, not to mention Shiism. To walk through these neighbourhoods is to learn the meaning of tolerance. What Salman Rushdie says of Bombay – a metropolis in which the mulitiplicity of interwoven beliefs and cultures curiously creates a remarkably secular atmosphere (1993:26) - is Ebrahim's experience of Dar. The city did not experience the after-effects of the Zanzibar Revolution, nor have there been any race riots since 1964. The city no longer erupts into violence, unlike Nairobi where the African masses sometimes attack Indian street corner shops. Here neighbourhoods are the picture of a divided world, but where convivencia, the fact of living together without necessarily liking one another, has been part of the landscape for a long time.

Ebrahim doesn't like wandering in Kariakoo. He needs to cross Mnazi Mmoja, to walk the Indian streets, along the walls of the Shiite mosque, to reach the Askari roundabout, to take Zanaki Street down to the harbour opposite the Catholic Cathedral and the building of the White Fathers, formerly the Sultan's harem. Ebrahim once told me that he considered the cathedral to be one of Dar's most beautiful buildings. It cuts a fine figure; but in my humble opinion, the Shiite mosque is not too bad either.

September 13, 1995

During my first visit, when the project of writing this book took shape, I faced an unprecedented difficulty: finding Ebrahim's house. Today, it is part of my mental geography of Dar, where it has a central position. All my Tanzanian colleagues whom I informed about the project and my visits asked for Ebrahim's address. In a city for which maps are either impossible to find or twenty years old, finding a house is i*'t always easy. It's his father's house. He shares the house. His father is also a poet; he went to the University of Al Azhar. He is held in high esteem by the Muslim community.*

During this first interview I was unaware of the importance of Ebrahim's father. On my return a month later, having heard that Jean-Claude Penrad's work was progressing, I contacted him. He was busy editing the film *Maulidi ya Hom* which he showed at the 1997 Metz Scientific Film Festival. This is how the film was presented in the programme:

> *In Zanzibar, Tanzania, a Muslim ritual is practised, called Maulidi ya Hom, which comes from Sufi Muslim tradition. Formerly associated with mortification practices that have since been abandoned, it has survived in the countryside. It is performed at the request of persons wishing to mark an important event in their personal, family or community life with the aim of attracting divine blessing. Reciting from the Koran, chants about the life of the Prophet Mohammed, percussion rhythms and female voices accompany the swaying, performing figures, who reach ecstatic divine proximity through oblivion of terrestrial perceptions. The representation evolves towards a joyous outcome in keeping with the religious theme.*

In this film one of the leaders of the liturgy is Ebrahim Hussein's eldest brother, who is a computer scientist. Jean-Claude Penrad explained to me the importance of Ebrahim's family, who introduced the brotherhood of Shadhliya to the continent. The brotherhood supported the trade between the Zanzibari tax collectors and the people of Kilwa. Ebrahim's grandfather donated the Swahili bed that decorates the hall devoted to Kilwa in the Tanzania National Museum. This world is not unknown to Ebrahim. He didn't return to Kilwa and declined the offer to accompany me there, but in 1995 he was in contact with Kilwa via the salt-trade. Transportation difficulties, the competition of Indian salt and the collapse of Zaire (which was their main market), ruined this enterprise.

September 14, 1995

Ebrahim talks non-stop. As usual, we head downtown through the Indian quarter. In front of the Shiite mosque he talks to me of Behrangi. He translated one of his narratives into Kiswahili. He tells me: "These people like black. Who are these people? Persians, Shiites: in short, The Shirazi, the mythical ancestors of the Swahili. Behrangi was one of them: he was a communist, but wrote in Persian and his little fish is black?" I ask him what he thinks of Salman Rushdie. He tells me he is also one of them: admittedly the character Salman the Persian is the one who brought down the wrath of the Ayatollahs on Salman Rushdie. However, not being Persian, Iranian or even a Shiite writer, Salman Rushdie belongs to that Indo-Muslim world to which Islam went via Iran which coloured it in its own way. Ebrahim says nothing against Salman Rushdie in 1995 but makes it understood that he condemns the latter's provocative behaviour, even though he thinks that poetic licence does exist.

During my last visit in 1997, he spontaneously mentioned Rushdie and his attitude. On each of my visits I penetrated deeper into the compound; that is to say into the inner courtyard. It is a modest perpend house with a corrugated-iron roof. There is a well. Ebrahim's room opens onto a corridor in which salt was stored in 1995. I have never found Ebrahim in the courtyard, but almost always a half-sister or half-brother. Ebrahim's mother is dead; his father has remarried. The girls, often in *baibuis* would welcome me very warmly: they seemed delighted that their brother received visitors. Were they secretly relieved to see that he could go out? That he could smile? I never saw his father in the courtyard. Professor T. S. Sengo, one of the major Tanzanian critics, former director of the University's Kiswahili Research Institute, offered to introduce me to Ebrahim's father. I accepted the offer, but before the planned appointment I was given the opportunity of meeting Sheikh Nouredin.

During one of my visits a young man - I found out later that he was one of the Sheikh's pupils - let me into the house – it was the only time I entered it. He invited me into a room that must have been the office or library. The walls were covered with books written in Arabic; the Sheikh arrived and we exchanged a few common places. Ebrahim entered, sat down and struck up a conversation about Ngugi with me. I felt uncomfortable and took my leave of the Sheikh, thanking him for receiving me. Professor Sengo had spoken to me of this eminent man. Ebrahim has also mentioned his father several times: he admired his talent as a poet but disapproves of his casuistic finesse: how does one accept the notion of a "temporary" marriage?

In 1995 I met Professor Sengo several times. On the occasion of our first interview, in the company of a celebrated Kenyan Swahili poet, A. Sheikh Nabahany, he complained of the growing influence of the mainland people on the Swahili language, which according to him, should be distinguished from its coastal, and, probably, Muslim origins. Sengo is a Muslim militant, but a militant in the Swahili style, that is to say moderate. He expresses frankly the frustration of the coastal inhabitants who feel they have been left out.

There is no road to Kilwa suitable for motor vehicles during the rainy season. I took the only boat connecting Mtwara and Mikindani, from where the Kilwa caravans used to go down to Ruvuma and the Lakes. Today the voyage to Southern Tanzania is still long and difficult. There are good roads to the North and the South West; there are none to the South, to Kilwa where Ebrahim was born - and not in Lindi, as indicated in biographical notes. Lindi is the administrative city, the former German capital. Kilwa has been a Muslim enclave for centuries. During the thirteenth century there was a great palace and a mosque. In 1503 Vasco da Gama estimated that Kilwa had 12,000 inhabitants, and in 1517 Diego Barbosa admired the sculpted city gates. Shortly afterwards (in 1572) it was celebrated by Camoens in his Luciads. Results of excavations undertaken in Kilwa since the end of the fifties, presented in two volumes (Chittick, 1974), show almost uninterrupted occupation for more than ten centuries. Kilwa supplied rot-proof mangrove wood and exported sea-cucumbers to Asia, from which the Japanese made unusable shoes. Today, Kilwa is a sleepy town, and I was unable to visit. This isolation is one of the causes of frustration for the Southern and coastal inhabitants - those who reigned for ten centuries over this part of the continent.

Ebrahim does not share Sengo's militancy. He goes to pray at the mosque, but condemns the political manifestations of the religion. In Swahili, secular is translated by a circumlocution: that which does not mix religious and political principles. He also denounces the negligence and the mistrust which he believes his community - Muslims from the coast - has been subjected to by the government. He is sensitive to the criticisms repeatedly levelled at his community. One day he told me the story of a drawing competition organised by the Goethe Institute: Arabs beating Blacks everywhere. It hurt him.

September 15, 1995

I asked him: why isolate yourself? He told me: I am driven into a corner; there is no room for me. There are art schools and institutes everywhere, but people don't care a damn about art, they don't know what it means. And yet I write, I carry on, people don't believe it. And when someone from the outside world comes, I give him a text to show him that I am still working; to know what he thinks of it. One day a Japanese man came to see me: he thought I was dead, or that I was a one-legged old man. Ebrahim writes at home; he tells me that there are no teachers, no critics, no publishers and no readers. When one has seen something of the offices of the Tanzania Publishing House, one understands what Ebrahim means by saying that there are no real publishers. This, he tells me in the office of Walter Bgoya, who ran the Tanzania Publishing House but left there to set up his own publishing house.

Ebrahim is a defender of secularism: it is his understanding that this constitutional disposition must allow everybody to practise the religion of his choice. He does not say it; but for me it is something very positive, inherited from Mwalimu Nyerere's politics. Walks in the streets of Dar show evidence of this shared existence. There is a Masonic temple next to the Lutheran cathedral; I am not even counting the number of mosques. As I said during a walk with Ebrahim: "There are many mosques". He agreed, adding: "And many Tartuffes". There is a thin line between militants like Sengo and those who don't understand that the people from the coast should be treated better than they are and that one should avoid rejecting them. One evening Ebrahim told me: "The Mwalimu has two bedside books: the Bible and the Arusha Declaration, so Sengo certainly has the right to his own ideas"

September, 21, 1995
> *Ebrahim talks to me about his two grandfathers. On his father's side, the Imam of Kilwa did not support nationalists. He gave a piece of land to the English who turned it into an airport, and a bed which can still be seen in the Museum. His grandfather on his mother's side was a fervent TANU militant. It was he who helped Ebrahim during his militant years in the village. Mashetani's dedication bears witness to it:* Kwa marehemu babu: *in memory of my grandfather.*

His grandfather had nothing to show for it. At the end of his life he was entitled to two kilograms of sugar which Ebrahim fetched for him.

The walks always took the same route in 1995 and during my last visit in April 1997. Following an unchanging itinerary we went downtown in search of a café. Ebrahim wanted a café with a European feel to it. It reminded him of his years in Berlin at the beginning of the seventies which he kept referring to. He spent several years there. He had a flat and a girlfriend who also had her own flat. He could go to West Berlin and associate with people from the drama world described by Heiner Muller in his memories of his years in the Berliner Ensemble; there he reflected on Hamlet and on Shakespeare (Muller, 1996: 207-232).

These were years of creativity for artists. They were stimulated by external constraints which forced them to be crafty, to conceal. It led them to use riddles, just as Ebrahim would some time later. He could go to the Berliner Ensemble to see Brecht's plays. He learnt to view the world with the distance which Brecht himself did not always keep in real life, but which his plays allude to.

Industry is a threat to live performance. Ebrahim is vividly conscious of the impact of industry on culture in Tanzania, especially video. The latter signals the advent of the industrial ability to reproduce mimetic works of fiction. Walter Benjamin had understood it, but here it was the death of cinema, and to an extent, the theatre. There are no more cinemas in Dar; only video rental shops. Occassionally, scrawled on some wall, posters invite one to participate in a *taarab* competition.

For a long time there was no television in Tanzania. The president thought it useless for a country as poor as his own. Only the Zanzibaris did not deny themselves this luxury. For the past few years Dar has had four television stations. Obscene satellite dishes reach for the sky to collect showers of nonsense. They broadcast American or Kenyan soap operas (at least the latter are in Kiswahili) and sometimes Tanzanian shows. In September 1995 the screens were filled with the crowning of Miss Tanzania. On this occasion Ebrahim explained to me the difference between *urembo*, the beauty of the contestants, that of the screen and of appearance, and *wema*, the beauty that comes from inside. His ideal is this interior beauty.

The more I read Ebrahim, the more I understand his interest in Brecht: I will explain it in the next chapter. In a world of rapid movement, he who wants to understand, has to provide himself with instruments to connect culture and politics. But he must not turn this method of analysis into the basis for a new religion. These social dynamics carried by the heterogeneous language of the theatre - which allows one to make collages between old Swahili poetry, language used on the streets and the new standard language - is what interests him. He was lucky to have had Joachim Fiebach as a professor.

I asked him several times why he did not want to travel any more. The French Embassy's Cultural Services had invited him to France a few years ago, but he did not go. He explained to me that he was scared of having his passport confiscated at the border. He was referring to the Kenyan incident which could have turned out very badly. And yet Kenya, where he is certainly not *persona grata* today, is not the whole of Africa, and it was the only neighbouring country which could have offered him a post worthy of his stature, and which would have kept him in contact with the Swahili community.

By his behaviour Ebrahim has closed this door. Because of his dislike of Kenya, he does not even want to collect his royalties. His books are sold in Kenya and can be found in all bookstores. In Tanzania this is no longer the case. In Nairobi I met the manager of Oxford University Press. He told me that Ebrahim's works had a wide circulation, but that the money from them was lying dormant in a bank and was devaluing steadily, following the downward slide of the Kenyan economy.

He has also taken a dislike for his former University colleagues and is now all alone.

September 21, 1995

Today he sells some salt, writes some poems, reads. On the door of the house is written chumvi safi, *quality salt. He tells me: they keep on saying that I'm hiding: it's not true, I'm working ... Nobody wanted to listen to my lectures, nobody wanted to understand Brecht.*

We then have a discussion about the meaning of the word plebeijsch, *about the dialectic of the verb in Kiswahili. The* plebeijsch *concept means the dialectic richness of the point of view of those that are dominated, a possibility which also exists in Kiswahili to transform viewpoints by adding suffixes to the root. There is a dialectic in the words, in the form of the words themselves. Ebrahim often comes back to that. To write a poem he starts with forms and rhythms; the contents, the message comes afterwards. He often mimes the rhythms he perceives. He writes* diwani, *poems about his mother who died two years ago; he wrote a play about AIDS, but doesn't want to publish it: it needs to be compressed ... He doesn't want to publish.*

He tells me that people don't understand anything about literature, have never read anything, don't know other writers and spend their time criticizing him. What matters to him is Brecht, his play on words, his creativity.

He's not a good Muslim, but he doesn't reject this world; he's from Malindi, where his family on his mother's side came from, from a popular Swahili Islam, open and festive.

He complains about not being able to find a job after 50. Yet he found a job in Nairobi, but he put himself into a delicate situation with the Kenyan government. In truth, he needs Kariakoo – its dialect, its market, its streets, its baraza, its coffee vendors, and the libraries of the foreign cultural centres.

Speaking about retribution, which he used as a theme for his last play, he asks me: what have we done to deserve separation, lack of love? Our friend Sengo can't understand that: it's not part of his worldview. Ebrahim has a tragic conception of existence, an acute sense of dignity, of values, of their derisive nature. But also of their importance, and a radical pessimism concerning this society where everything is corrupt: politics, education, values. He no longer has any desire to teach in the kingdom of Miss Tanzania; there is no more room for him. The only faith he has left is in his art.

He could travel - he has a passport and he gets invitations. He has sentenced himself to a sort of internal exile. Then he tells me - it's up to me to believe it - that others have condemned him to it. According to him, he has been trapped by the fathers, his own, Mwalimu, Baba wa Taifa, (the Father of the Nation). Abandoned by women, his own, his mother, his daughter who tells him that one writer in a family is enough, the other women he can't marry for lack of money. Surrounded by female colleagues: Penina, Amandina; the women's conference in Beijing; the Pope, on a visit to Nairobi at the same time...

2
Writing for the theatre

Ebrahim Hussein is known first and foremost as a dramatist; he is also a theorist and a teacher who has left us a collection of theoretical texts on the theatre, which form the framework of his theatrical universe. The central theme of his research is the origin of African theatre. Ebrahim Hussein is a child of his time: he belongs to the generation that celebrated its 18th birthday in 1961.

In his thesis he describes the literature course taught in the schools at that time: only English theatre was included. There were no East-African authors; Kiswahili theatre did not exist as an autonomous genre. The European colonies, or white communities, had their theatre in Nairobi and Dar. Amateur companies, including many colonials, defended the repertoire. All in all, as in West Africa, theatre existed in schools as a literary genre and in colonial circles as a social practice. The English theatre of Nairobi is still in existence although its actors and audiences are Kenyan today. Dar es Salaam's Little Theatre is still in existence but has had no company since the sixties. Theatre in the schools, whether European or Asian, was a minority cultural activity linked to extramural activities. There were schools for Asians, for Europeans and for Africans. The school system was not unified: Asians performed plays for Asians, in the same way as Europeans did for Europeans, whereas Africans continued to perform plays in English for the African elite.

> *The Little Theatre that opened in Oyster Bay, was to the European community in Oyster Bay what the Indo-Tanzania Cultural Centre was to the Asians in Upanga. The effect of British drawing room drama, within schools and outside, and Asian (Indian) drama; performance delivered in foreign languages, enacted by foreigners was an important one. The African elite soon accepted this form of art as 'the' form of drama despite the fact that it was foreign to Tanzania and to East Africa as a whole (Hussein, 1975).*

Social reality goes beyond the limits of the stage; with a little imagination, a few young Tanzanian spectators or Shakespeare readers must have thought that their society, jolting through a difficult birth, had something which could attract theatre. Ebrahim Hussein was one of them. He was confronted by the reasoning of his generation: theatre must exist in Africa, that expression of human genius should not be absent from Africa. Ebrahim Hussein's sense of history is too well developed for him to fall into the *'we too, have'* discourse, popular during the first decades of independence, all the more so because the identity 'we' is to be treated with caution, as we shall see in Chapter 4. A debate on the existence of theatre in Africa was raging in the west. The diffusion of the notion of theatricality *(theatre without text),* according to Barthes, suited many people. The only problem was that the liveliest and most original theatre in Africa was performed through texts. Wole Soyinka received the Nobel Prize for drama texts known by all Nigerians.

Theatre and Popular Traditions

A sense of history is expressed through the knowledge of popular entertainment practices. For example, the tom-tom on parade, a percussion brass band, *bendi ngoma,* imitates the colonial army but subtly introduces scorn into this mimicry. This form of entertainment has been studied by historian, Terence Ranger, who analysed the components of interest for the practice of this apparently innocuous activity, which was prohibited during the colonial era. This public demonstration by Swahili groups, stemming from traditional practices of musical and sparring matches, was seen as a threat by the authorities who prohibited these meetings during the thirties. Ebrahim Hussein fully understands that these parades are a form of defiance; a social act - African performance expressing its veiled refusal to be dominated. Only a procession, even with song and dance, is not a play; there is no narrative and no story is told.

> *In fact we were greatly surprised by the bendi. A dance-style that seemed to be pure entertainment turned out to be deeply rooted in culture; original and adaptable. In this sense the bendi ngoma can be considered a metaphor for many other aspects of East African contemporary culture which are usually explained in terms of*

> *Europeanisation. It is true that nothing seems more European than the bendi. Yet this brass-band tradition has its origins outside of Europe. Some of these influences were still active in nineteenth century Africa: the apparent exoticism of the dance exercises, and, the mimed combats, derived from the traditions of dance duels from the Swahili coast. With or without direct European influence the African societies from the East coast reacted to the impact of the modern world and it is important to distinguish between their own creative response and what was imposed by European agents* (Ranger 1975:164).

Amongst the forms of popular entertainment listed by Ebrahim Hussein are *taarab* shows, song recitals interrupted by comical playlets which are the main form of entertainment in Zanzibar and the Swahili coast community. A *taarab* orchestra has about a dozen musicians:

> *Male ensembles featured a solo singer with four or five male singers in a chorus, a qanum (trapezoidal board zither) ud (short-necked plucked lute) nay (oblique blown flute), violin and a riqq (small round frame drum with metal jingles). Female groups were more percussion oriented, including, besides the singers, at least one darabukka, more than one tar (large frame drum with metal jingles, closely associated with the music of the harem) a riqq, and a lone melody instrument, the ud* (Topp-Fargion, 1997:60-61).

The custom is to interrupt the recital with a theatrical interlude: the title is provided and its written outlines are usually the actors' only guidelines: *taarab* and theatre, *kichekesho* (literally: comic interlude, plural: *vichekesho*), thus often go together.

A *taarab* evening is an event, and the show follows a complex protocol. The songs, often known by all and dealing with the hackneyed themes of love and jealousy, are often parodied during the comic interlude. The strength of the *taarab* also came from Siti Binti Saad's personality, a great singer and actress who turned her recitals into true moments of theatrical expression. This was noticed by her admirers: in his biography of Siti, Shaaban Robert highlights this aspect of her career; she was a *"mwimbaji na mwigizaji"*: "a singer and an actress" (Shaaban, 1952:40).

She introduced a form of Indian dance and mime into taarab performances which, in Zanzibar, became known as natiki (possibly from the general Hindi term for dance, natak) or nachi Natiki which was later replaced by the performance of popular plays – "Michezo ya kuigiza" in Kiswahili (Topp-Fargion, 1997:61).

Similarly, Siti's principal heir, Bakari Abeid, who dominated the *taarab* stage throughout the sixties, and who was still living in Kariakoo in 1997, was known for his acting as well as his singing qualities.

Ebrahim Hussein is susceptible to these dimensions of a performance in Kiswahili which involve actors and which come close to a form of drama, that is, text associated with image by means of body language.

In his thesis Hussein explains that *taarab* and *vichekesho* are an integral artistic form which developed in Zanzibar, but *vichekesho* can also be performed without the *taarab*. Such is the case in the plays of the drama group of the textile factories of Peter Saimanga (Hussein, 1975:98). This form was influenced by school theatre:

The "vichekesho na taarabu" tradition is continued by Bakari Abeid in Zanzibar. From there it spread to the mainland, first to Tanga then Dodoma and Dar es Salaam. The development of vichekesho during all this time was independent of drama in educational institutions and of both the British and the Asian theatre, although there might have been some influence of these on the former (Hussein, 1975:102).

The *taarab* together with the *kichekesho* "is like concert party"; this is what Ebrahim Hussein told me the first time I met him in 1984, during an assignment at the University of Dar es Salaam where he occupied the chair of theatre studies. The concert party is a form of narrative show, an oral tradition which is acted and sung, offering stories from contemporary urban life: stories about families in the city (Ricard, 1987). I had written a paper on this subject and Hussein knew my work. Comparing the two genres with these few words he made it clear to me that the *taarab* was not merely a type of song recital, but also a form of drama, telling everyday stories. Stories that are seldom analysed, seldom commented on, seldom mentioned. I watched hours of *taarab* in the studios of Television Zanzibar. The dramatic interludes were not recorded: they were too everyday, too commonplace. In the archives of a *taarab* group, Janet Topp-Fargion collected the outlines of plays. They are placed before and after the interval, contain few characters and portray young people, their problems at work and in their love-life.

Mwimbaji maarufu wa Zanzibar katika miaka hiyo alikuwa Bakari Abeid, ambaye alizaliwa Agosti 25, mwaka 1933 kisiwani Pemba. Akielezea juu ya umuhimu wa mchezo wa kuigiza, Bakari alisema: "Unawafanya watu wacheke katika ukweli wa maisha, lakini wakati huo huo unawaelekeza wafuate tabia njema katika kazi na starehe ya mapumziko...". Ilikuwa ni kawaida kwa kila mwimbaji kuona kuwa kuiga ndio ustadi wa kuimba. Siku hizi nafasi ipo ya kuimba katika uasili wetu" (Khatib, 1992:26).

In those years, the greatest singer in Zanzibar was Bakari Abeid, who was born on 25 August 1933, on the island of Pemba. Explaining the importance of these shows. Bakari said: "You make people laugh about the truths of life, but at the same time direct them to keep up good habits at work and while relaxing and enjoying themselves...". It was unusual for every singer to believe that acting was really the height of art. These days there is room for singing as part of our tradition.

These popular practices originate from the coastal cultures, the Waswahili. If there are elements for Tanzanian theatre, one must also look for them in the representation of oral narratives, and in the staging of these recitals. Oral literature provides appropriate indications. Thus, Ebrahim Hussein observes that in the first collection of Swahili short stories (Steere, 1870) the story - or rather the narrative - of Sultan Majnuni, contains indications about spectator participation which could indicate that it was performed as a play.

The most curious thing in this collection is perhaps the latter part of the tale of Sultan Majnuni where everyone present joins in singing the verses, if they may be so called, which, besides are not in Kiswahili. (Steere, 1970:VII)

The storyteller addresses his public and invites them to respond by playing the game of which they are a part. The spontaneous manifestations of popular culture or folklore, a term we could use if it had not taken on a pejorative meaning, offers many examples of this truly theatrical alliance of word and image. That is what the young Hussein turns to when he tries to root theatrical expression in Tanzanian culture.

Another channel is that of the poetic traditions of the peoples of the interior of the country – and, particularly, of the Great Lakes. The heroic recitals, not only of the *Bahima*, but also of the *Bahaya* or the *Bakerebe*, are, in their way, theatre performances. The story teller is a true comedian expressing himself as much with his words as with his body. The heroic reciting of the Bahima of Ankole is a type of performance: *"the execution of the poem is the poem"* (Valery, 1960:1350). Without a mimesis of the action being intended, the narrator is, nonetheless, the author of a certain body language accompanying a text which is sometimes declaimed in the first person, as in the old Basotho songs which Casalis described so well.

Ethnological literature offers numerous examples of these situations, the potential of which was used in the sixties by another East African writer, Okot p'Bitek, in his *Song of Lawino* (p'Bitek, 1966). The cultures of the Great Lakes and the Bantu peoples of Central Africa are familiar with heroic recital, the declamation of bards, which is certainly a form of theatrical expression, i.e. mixing word and gesture - however slight. Mukotani Rugyendo tries to create a show consisting of a reconstituted poetry joust - *The Contest* (1977). Unfortunately, in my opinion, the written English of these poems is far removed from the force and vivacity they would have if written in an African tongue; even in translation the author does not measure up to the bards he is trying to emulate in written form. The experience comes to a sudden end.

The coast cultures also have their heroic declamation, like that of Fumo Lyongo (Mulokozi, Sengo: 1995), to the north of the Swahili sphere: Fumo Lyongo would thus be a hero from the interior of the continent. Performed speech is part of Swahili culture. Ebrahim Hussein is himself an actor; he enacted the poem *Ngoma na Vailini* (Drum Versus the Violin, Abdulaziz, 1979:104) himself on the stage of the university theatre.

Singing and dancing are forms of Swahili entertainment leading us into the universe of theatre, even if they are not the canonical forms thereof. Ebrahim Hussein views the theatre through the eyes of a playwright and an actor: he has a great reputation as an actor. Performance, staging and theatre are notions that are very close in his oeuvre, and which he does not separate from poetry. He is hostile to the confusion between ritual and theatre: if heroic recitation is a form of show, it is not a ritual form: speech is performed, power is also portrayed on stage.

These are not religious moments, but they celebrate texts which are cultural monuments. In drama, there is narrative, story, memory, personal identity: a personal signature, an unmistakable voice, a kind of critic in the Barthesian sense. Ebrahim Hussein is not a manufacturer of myths. We do not find the proposition in his writing that celebrations like initiation rites are forms of drama. He later said this very clearly at a conference on Ngugi, and in a text which would serve as a preface to the translation of his play *Arusi*.

Political theatre

In coast cultures one should distinguish between the old culture, that of wedding festivals, the *taarab* of feasts where these practices are reinterpreted, and of their transformation into expression types, or even into shows, under the influence of urbanisation and emigration. We have already mentioned the innovations brought to the *taarab* by Bakari Abeid. The invention of dramatic forms closer to 'European' theatre seems to go hand in hand with the creation of politically and union-driven organisations.

The playlet - the *kichekesho* - which served as a comic interlude during *taarab* evenings becomes a genre in its own right. The textile workers turn it into an 'anti-capitalist', conscience-awakening instrument, says Fiebach (1993) in an article on Tanzanian theatre. Thus, alongside entertainment shows associated with Swahili culture, a politically committed genre is created in Kiswahili:

The vichekesho (comic skits) of the seventies, after the Arusha Declaration, that introduced Ujamaa, became the theatre of the working class. Through the vichekesho the Tanzanian workers rallied behind socialism and exposed the capitalist forces responsible for their exploitation (Mlama, 1991:97- 98).

Here are a few basic *vichekesho* frameworks performed after the Arusha Declaration and belonging to this form of politically militant theatre:

·· *Adui ujinga (illiteracy is the enemy)*: an illiterate father is deceived by his daughter who claims that a letter she has received from a lover is a school report.

·· *Ulanguzi (racketeering)*: a man finds ways of making money, and profits quickly through shady activities. He is apprehended one day when he boasts about his activities to a group of people who include the law.

·· *Kuku na mayai (chicken and eggs)*: a man divorces his wife and soon after leaves town. He remarries in his new town and after a long stay there returns to his old town where he discovers that his new wife and the old one are mother and daughter.

·· *Meneja mhujumu (the embezzling manager)*: a manager of a corporation uses public funds recklessly and for his own personal interests. When he is found out, he commits suicide.

·· *Namtaka mume afisa (I want an officer husband)*: an ambitious girl turns down many suitors because she aims to marry a man with a high position. A cleaner pretending to be a worker in an office turns up one day, and the girl agrees to marry him. The pretence is unmasked when the wife finds the husband sweeping at the market place and a fight ensues (Lihamba, 1985:500-502).

At the same time as drama was added to the curriculum, with themes related to popular education, a university drama programme was put in place, along the lines of drama schools - whereby drama was attached to the other branches of university teaching. From the start, Hussein has been associated with this type of teaching which calls on lecturers from East Germany (J. Fiebach), from America (H. Shore). Stage professionals and playwrights have to be trained; drama is a separate discipline in secondary education, explaining its presence in a university. Pupils have to be exposed to the grand repertoire, following a principle which has proved its efficiency at the Drama School of the University of Ibadan (Ricard, 1972).

> *Between 1967 and 1986, there have only been about six productions of European plays by a Tanzanian cast for a Tanzanian audience. These were: The Trojan Women (University Theatre Department, 1968); The Vulture, an adaptation of Schwartz's The Dragon (University Theatre Department, 1968); Nyerere's Swahili translation of Shakespeare's The Merchant of Venice (University Theatre Department, 1969); Mushi's Swahili Traslation of Sophocles' Oedipus (Butimba college of Art, 1983); Chekov's The Bear (University Theatre Department, 1969) and Brecht's The Measures Taken (University Theatre Department, 1976) (Mlama, 1991:99).*

The notion of drama development, which Hussein used as a subject for his doctoral thesis, is fully applied here: the performances change according to political contexts, new forms are created and some, like the *kichekesho*, are close to known drama forms in the rest of the world, like agitprop, or politically militant theatre.

Unlike his colleagues from West Africa, Ebrahim Hussein does not put the question about the language of expression because he considers it resolved. The whole debate, pursued particularly in Nigeria, on 'African theatre' and the 'theatricality' of African cultures, can also be read as an effort to compensate, by language and image, for the death of African speech. In other words, refusing, practically, to write in an African language despite all the rhetorical denials. In the West the theoretical necessity is all the more imperious as, in practice, there is no hope.

That is not the problem encountered by Hussein at all: he creates in a language that everyone understands, and he does not need to mask the radical novelty of his creations with a veil of artificial cultural continuity. His reflection on the theatre has, therefore, to be read as a rupture with that of his anglophone colleagues of the same generation. John Rugenda and Ngugi wa Thiong'o can read his works, for knowledge of **Kiswahili is widespread** in East Africa, but they do not write in Kiswahili, and probably would not be able to do so. It is not enough to speak and understand a language to write in it. Ebrahim Hussein's oeuvre is radically new since it can be situated, from the outset, in the field of the most contemporary writing. At the same time, it is written in an African language, and tries to theorise this new situation in black Africa. His theoretical work is, first of all, an examination of theatrical elements present in Swahili and Tanzanian culture. Including certainly the cultures of the Great Lakes - those of the great heroic recitals - followed by a reflection, based on this inventory, on the elements likely to be used again in the perspective of drama of cultural and political liberation, which continues the tradition of the Arusha Declaration.

The 'popular' notion (*plebejisch* is the German word Ebrahim Hussein uses) enables one to grasp the creative contradiction between the inventory to which the writer of a thesis devotes himself, and the mobilisation anticipated by the author. People like to amuse themselves by dancing, but dances can also be calls for liberation. Such is the meaning of the *bendi ngoma*. Is the comic strength of the *vichekesho* playlets a call for liberation, for struggle against colonial or capitalist domination? It was at one time, but if socialism becomes the 'religion of the state' these theatrical rites will be too much in harmony with the official ideology.

Ebrahim Hussein, poet and actor, is conscious of the contradictions of popular art, which is not always an art of protest, but which can also celebrate power: a song of praise is as important as a poetic joust. In this way, the Arusha Declaration gave rise to the development of a verbal genre originating from the Wagogo tradition (Mnyampala, 1995). The *ngonjera* opens with a pedagogical aim, illustrating socialist principles and teaching good Kiswahili. The name of Mathias Mnyampala, a nationalistic militant and 'organic' intellectual of the Wagogo, is associated with this type of poetry in dialogue form, which opposes two characters discussing the meaning of socialist principles. One of them knows what it is about and explains it to his interlocutor.

The *ngonjera* slowly changed into a dramatic performance and became a type of drama: authors like Penina Mhando composed *ngonjera*, as did poets and novelists like Euphrase Kezilahabi. The *ngonjera* prospered in the euphoria that followed the Arusha

Declaration. However, the genre fell victim to the disenchantment of the last years of the sixties with the questioning of socialism, under pressure of the facts and of the vagueness of the debates. In the seventies, the *ngonjera* became a genre mostly practised by school drama companies who appreciated its static and didactic character.

Popular poetry and drama, of which Ebrahim Hussein tried to grasp the dramatic and spectacular potentialities, becomes a politically militant art in the service of a political project. We enter the world of political cant and of ready-made formulae: the jujube tree (*mkunazi*) of *Jogoo kijijini* will be a reaction full of refined sap to these bone-dry speeches.

Islam and drama

In a famous novella, *La Busca de Averroes*, J. L. Borges recounts the difficult search of Averroes, the translator of Aristotle's *Poetics*, who imagined, according to Renan, who is quoted in an epigraph, *"that tragedy is nothing other than the art of praising"* (Borges, 1962:105). The Islamic tradition did not offer the translator any example of the representative mimesis the Greek philosopher deals with, and upon which our author has been reflecting endlessly. Ebrahim Hussein comes from an old Muslim family, we know that his grandfather was an Imam in Kilwa. He grew up in the Sunni Islam of his father, in the Shadhalia brotherhood with which his family is associated. The Imam is known for having established this brotherhood in Kiiwa at the beginning of the century.

This port has always been a point of contact between the two great Islamic traditions. Shiism has been there for a long time. Certainly, in the Sunni Islam Ebrahim grew up in, there is no room for the theatre, be it tragedy or comedy. On the other hand, there is room for poetry, for the poetic exaltation of the *sufis*, for the *dhikr* liturgies, those litany-like scansions accompanied rhythmically by the whole body of the brotherhood's followers. Theatre is something completely different. Ebrahim Hussein appreciates the novelty of his project, situated outside religion and not to be confused with it. For him, theatre, which is not a ludic activity, but in fact a search for fundamental truth, has its own logic. Theatre sets forces in motion, which may surpass it. He draws from the same sources as the trance; but it is up to the dramatist to control the energies he sets free.

The taarab and the trance

The trance of the followers of the brotherhood, surrounded by the community of followers, is an example of these liberations. What is more theatrical than these whirling dervishes, these gesticulated prayers that Ebrahim Hussein must have known (Penrad, 1997). These practices are 'inventions of the theatre' and are part of Ebrahim's theoretical and practical horizon. He probably saw the Shiites celebrating the martyr of Hussein, described in Sacleux ethnological dictionary (1891). Moreover, as I have indicated, he does not merely know the theatre as a reader and a playwright; he practices drama as an actor. He knows what release of energy is demanded of the player and to what extent the regulars of these trance seances are masters in controlling these forces.

His vision of theatre and its practice is not merely intellectual: he also has physical knowledge of it. The *dhikr* seances, of incantatory recitals, generating trances, are not rites but collective prayer practices. Word and gesture are associated to produce a semi-conscious state where more attention is paid to the divine; these are merely techniques to get closer to God. Could one not say by transposition that the scenic representation is the trap in which the author wants to try to catch the king's conscience, or the spectator's?

As Hamlet says: *The play is the thing wherein I will catch the conscience of the king.* Like Brecht, Shakespeare is constantly present on our author's horizon. We know that Shakespeare is present in Swahili literature programmes, a tradition emanating from President Nyerere, the Mwalimu. To the pupils, Ebrahim Hussein is the other playwright, published by the same publisher as Shakespeare. Competition is obviously tough; but Ali Mazrui, a very incisive analyst of Swahili culture, points out that the incorporation of Shakespeare into the Swahili culture is the sign of a divided identity. To exorcise this domination, perhaps may be all that is left to them.

The publication of Julius Nyerere's Swahili translation of Shakespeare's Julius Caesar occurred close to the emergence of Kenya as an independent nation. No one realised at the time that Nyerere's translation of the English bard would one day be taught as part of Swahili literature in Kenyan schools. Is this part of what Edward Said, the Palestinian man of letters, has explored in his book 'Culture and imperialism'? Is the African-self still at odds with his own colonised other? In the fields of both language and literature, the European other occupies the mind of the African self with post-colonial stubbornness (Mazrui, 1995).

Brecht

Popular forms like *taarab* evenings, *vichekesho*, incantatory pratices like the *dhikr*, offer a whole palette of entertainment none of which shows any clear conformity with the school or university theatre model which had been awarded prizes in the competitions Hussein had attended. During the sixties, up to 1966, all of these forms seemed very far removed from each other: an art theory was needed which could use popular forms for cultural and political liberation. It would be Brecht's theory, presented by J. Fiebach, professor of drama at the university where he staged *Kinjeketile* in 1969.

It would be too simple to go no further than a political reading of what attracted Brecht. Co-operation with the German Democratic Republic was not the most important thing. Brecht's poetry and theoretical works offered answers to the questions which young African dramatists of those years were asking themselves. Wole Soyinka was one of the first to be susceptible to it. Brecht paid a lot of attention to the popular forms of entertainment, be it fairground theatre, cinema or songs. His theatre language will be a composite fabrication, like the Kiswahili of our author, who voluntarily chose to write standard Kiswahili.

Robert Philipson notes the ease with which Hussein reproduces every day language from his very first plays. He can mix poetic forms (for example elisions) with words borrowed from English, typical of pupil and student language, and in these collages he proves how good an ear he has for the spoken language.

Brecht's interest in popular narratives, tales and apologues, notably from the Orient, is well known. This receptiveness to folklore brings him close to the writers from the new African countries who know that oral narratives are often their spectators' first, and sometimes only, experience of verbal art. The attention paid to these narratives is aimed at the narrative procedures: the beginning, the incompleteness, the circularity break the linear progression of the Aristotelian narrative. Brecht is at ease in the universe of the Oriental tale, just as Ebrahim Hussein is.

The attraction to liberation of form is not to be dissociated from the concern of appealing to the spectator's or listener's reflection. Tales, narratives are never gratuitous: this intellectualism quite suits Ebrahim Hussein. In an article which appeared in 1975, but which was written several years earlier, Fiebach insists on Brecht's importance to Africa. He shows the contribution of Brecht's historical and materialistic method to theatre, the necessity to contextualise the problems in an historical sense, and to participate in the movement of political liberation. He blames some plays for not making the comprehension of the processes they refer to more accessible when examined from a Brechtian point of view. Wole Soyinka's play, *Kongi's Harvest* (1966) is judged as follows:

> *Soyinka has not even indicated what social forces have put Kongi where he is now or what social forces might be able to depose him and overcome the contradictions and shortcomings...since it lacks a concrete social structure that may, as a model, relate to reality, it does not really help the spectator or reader to get an insight into specific African reality and, thus, does not really encourage him to step into this reality and, help transform it* (Fiebach, 1975:170).

These remarks make one of the first formulations of the criticism levelled at Wole Soyinka by the "orthodox" Marxists - those that the Nobel Prize winner, in sparkling form, would baptise the "leftocrats" in response to their pamphlets. To them it is not enough to show the world, or even to satirise it - it must be changed, or the roads leading to change must be indicated. Fortunately, Joachim Fiebach did not stop at these views of the role of the dramatic art and of Soyinka's art. The Nigerian's plays on political denunciation dating from the sixties have been forgotten, but *Kongi's Harvest* remains one of the figures of power in Africa, a figure against which it is still necessary to defend itself today. Wole Soyinka's play is still topical, and *that* is certainly an original way, true to art, to change the world, by imposing on the world its own terms of reference, for example, Ubu or Kongi.

Ebrahim Hussein also criticises drama theory based on an integrated vision of African society: that of Ngugi, at least in certain theoretical texts which confuse community rites and drama practice. Bakary Traoré's book on *Théâtre Négro-Africain et ses Fonctions Sociales* (1958), translated into English in 1975, offers a few general directions of study in a language which borrows a holistic vision, strongly integrated in African society, from sociology. It is, in fact, the best illustration of a drama theory influenced by "négritude"/black consciousness themes sharing a consensual vision of African society, enclosed in its specificity.

Hussein's research is a lot richer because it starts out from the practice of theatre in different groups and from their possible contradictions. In his thesis on Ebrahim Hussein, Philipson (1989) amalgamates all African theatre from the sixties and seventies and does not see that the link with tradition can be critical or tragic, rather than ceremonial and incantatory, as in negritude poetry. Ebrahim Hussein's heroes are already Hamlet and Galileo Galilei.

Ngugi, Ruganda

Ebrahim Hussein appreciates Ruganda's play, *The Burdens* (1972). He writes:

> *It is undoubtedly the best play to come out of Uganda. It is national drama that criticises, or rather shows, the beginning of class formation...It can be said the question of relevance in Uganda has meant plays written by an African* (Hussein, 1975:134-136).

The content of the plays was of secondary importance. Our author has written about theatre in East Africa: this regional perspective had meaning in his formative years, and up to the creation of the universities of Dar and Nairobi at the end of the sixties. He showed that theatre did not exist in this region before this period. He was particularly interested in Ngugi's oeuvre, which contained several plays from the start and to which he would often return. Later he followed the oeuvre of John Ruganda, the Ugandan dramatist who would become Ngugi's colleague in Nairobi in the seventies.

In Nairobi there may be a drama repertoire for the elite, for the *Wabenzi*, the Mercedez-Benz owners. All in all, the theatre takes on an original shape: an anglophone public, aspiring to the representation of its own social life. Ngugi rejects all of that: Limuru is thirty minutes from the centre of Nairobi and people live in miserable conditions in shanty towns while the city sparkles next door. In this city there are musicals in English, soap operas on television, a drama academy. The latter, curiously, has its seat in the French Cultural Centre, the only equipped theatre in the town centre open to cultural projects. Ruganda's plays have been staged there.

The history of this theatre is difficult to separate from its performance conditions. The domination exercised by Kenyan opulence on the means of cultural production has resulted in the principal author of Swahili theatre being totally unknown and never staged in the city, where hundreds of thousands of copies of his works are published.

Ngugi wa Thiong'o and John Ruganda are the two authors through whom Ebrahim Hussein best defines himself. Both have the notion of a regional theatre: Ngugi, the Kenyan Gikuyu, comes from the mountains and the forests; Ruganda, the Ugandan, the man from the central lakes, comes from a country which was the jewel in the crown of the British Empire before becoming hell under Amin. Hussein, the man from the coast, open to the outside world was, at the same time, the only one of the three to write in what became the language of that part of the continent. The tripartite space providing a framework for the imagination of our three dramatists can be defined thus: lake-mountain-coast.

In the John Ruganda play, *Echoes of Silence* (1986), the ecological duality between lake and mountain serves as a model for reflection on the history of East Africa. Ebrahim Hussein is from the coast: he looks towards the ocean in works such as *The Little Black Fish*, and *Mashetani*, whose hero sails around without knowing where he is headed. Ngugi wa Thiong'o has been marked by the mountain men and those of the forest, the *Mau Mau*, these warriors around whom he tries to build a revolutionary mythology by means of drama. Dedan Kimathi, *Mau-Mau* general, a man from the forest, must be the positive hero that *Kinjeketile*, the man from the water, could not quite be. Mountain and forest are places of resistance, while sea and river are places of imaginary liberation for Hussein.

It is John Ruganda who explicitly builds an oeuvre from these differences. The lake is a crossroads, a world of encounters where coastal interbreeding has not yet taken place. Revolutionary mythologies don't bloom there as they do close to the mountain, but the tragedies of history struck early, destroying the illusions of Independence more rapidly. In one of John Ruganda's last plays, *The Floods* (1980), the sudden rising of the lake's waters is used as a metaphor of the region's political catastrophes, from Amin's genocide (the word is indeed used) to the beginning of the seventies.

These reciprocal echoes of the works of the three dramatists form an East African literary field which is necessarily in the process of interpretation. In it, our author's oeuvre takes its place and builds up in tension, along with those of his East African compatriots. The closing of the border between Tanzania and Kenya in 1977, which is reflected in his works, and the war with Uganda at the end of the seventies, are major moments of crisis for the region and the oeuvre. Before then, Ebrahim Hussein felt that his oeuvre was not limited to Dar es Salaam. Yet, that is where it would be confined.

John Ruganda's work is remarkable for its treatment of language, and of dramatic construction. The clashes between characters, the rifts between couples preoccupied with dreams, fantasies and memories are rendered with great mastery of dramatic language, in the tradition of Edward Albee or Tenessee Williams. The outer world is that of a Uganda torn by civil wars, and the characters belong to the social elites of the first regimes to be ousted. John Ruganda writes an international English: did the Ugandan intellectual elite choose English without any compunction? Compared to Ngugi Wa Thiong'o - we know about his linguistic conversion in the mid-seventies and his preoccupation with producing popular drama in Gikuyu - and compared to Hussein who has never wanted to write in a language other than Kiswahili, there is great originality here.

In John Ruganda's work, the depth and violence of the dialogue, which stirs the characters' subconscious, commands interest. The Ugandan author does not question the language of drama; from the start he plunges into the stage language of the contemporary psychological, naturalist theatre which he handles much better than any of his African contemporaries, perhaps with the exception of Athol Fugard. His characters' dreams are situated in a world politically torn apart.

In his last play, *Kwenye Ukingo wa Thym*, Ebrahim Hussein remembers John Ruganda's world and drama technique, mixing incursions into the subconscious with realistic dialogue; only, Hussein writes in Kiswahili. The Tanzanian author's literary project was an international one from the start, but he writes in an African language. In his 1995 conversations, Ebrahim Hussein was still referring to the importance of Ngugi's play, *This Time Tomorrow*, which had been published 30 years previously. This shows how attentive he is to the work of his East African compatriot, but it also shows the extent of his refusal to be blinded by political judgements of an oeuvre which is often of great simplism, notably the Gikuyu plays known to us through translation.

This Time Tomorrow is imagined as an inquiry in which numerous characters take part: it reveals their living conditions, it shows knowledge of the urban surroundings and doesn't idealise rural life. Young people are the heroes, as in Hussein's first plays, and in the dialogue this familiarity with the characters is evident. In his thesis, Hussein proposed an analysis in play-writing terms of the reasons for the effectiveness of the play, which he still quoted in admiration almost ten years later.

> *What has Uhuru brought to those who fought for it? The workers, the peasants and the forest fighters? The answer to the question is unmistakable in the play: nothing. More oppression, humiliation and dire poverty. Here the content is more clearly formulated. One reason for this is that the author abandons Aristotelian dramaturgy for epic. In fact, the story is written as a radio play, and the storyteller is a journalist who is working on an article that is to be published in a newspaper. We experience the story as narrated to*

us by one of the journalists, partly by following him to the scene of Uhuru market where he interviews the artisans and soup sellers, to get their angle. By using this form, the author has avoided verbosity and inaction that we found in The Black Hermit (Hussein, 1975: 154-155).

This Time Tomorrow is a pessimistic play; but it shows us a realistic picture of life in Nairobi through the journalist character's commentary and articles; it does not hide the Kenyan's prejudices, the obstacles created by an ethnic vision of social relations. The oeuvre is imbued with great lucidity on society, which is described in order to facilitate its change. A university had just been created in Nairobi; higher education would produce a new brand of men and women: beautiful illusions that would quickly be dissipated.

Theory and practice: the oeuvre in its context

Ebrahim Hussein conducted the research for his own thesis from 1970 to 1973, while the first thesis on his work, the work of Philipson, dates from 15 years later. These years of research, the beginning of the seventies, show a movement of separation between academic and creative activity. In parts, the thesis is an exercise in political cant, while theatrical testing is a formal and poetical innovation. From the end of the decade onwards, East Africa sinks deeper into crisis with the breaking up of the East African Community and the Ugandan war, and in the Eighties, with the failure of *ujamaa*.

At the same time the aesthetic question was clarified with the domination of Soyinka, and the possibility of an oeuvre which is African and anglophone at the same time: *Death and the King's Horseman*. This solution was not possible in East Africa where class, and race conflicts were more marked than in Nigeria. Ngugi wa Thiong'o was put under house arrest in 1977, and the social conflict intensified while aesthetic solutions became impoverished. In other words, in Africa Ebrahim Hussein will once again be given the position of marginal intellectual he occupied during his stay in East Berlin. He feels solidarity with Ngugi wa Thiong'o, confronted with authoritarian power, but he cannot accept the aesthetic and political solutions of his Kenyan colleagues.

For the Tanzanian author, who does not express it clearly, Ngugi's Marxism cannot serve as a theory of reference in the creation of an oeuvre. Ebrahim Hussein knows Brecht's theories extremely well, and he cannot accept seeing the drama field occupied by formulas as impoverishing as in Ngugi wa Thiongo's *Ngaahika Ndeenda* (I'll get married when I want to, 1980). Ebrahim Hussein experiences the contradictions in East African societies in an intense way. He tries to go beyond them by going deeper into a poetic vein, at the risk of being obscure. When he reaches a certain artistic maturity, the political debate becomes more Manichean and violent. As for him, he doesn't have the resource of exile: he cannot cut himself loose from his language and his world. Faced with the refusal to discuss or to stage his own works, he can only stay and suffer in silence, but does not resign himself to this sad fate.

In Kenya, armed with a materialistic theory of society and politics converted to Marxism and to a type of aesthetic populism, rallied to the cause of the landless peasants, Ngugi wa Thiong'o adheres to an idealistic language theory which is supposed to embody the essence of the village community. Drama would thus be the ritual ceremony displaying the founding myths of the *Gikuyu* society in a way that would delight British anthropologists (who were probably at the root of the theory, even if Ngugi objects to this hypothesis).

A strange coincidence which the Brechtian Hussein does not fail to mention: drama has nothing to do with ritual; drama is secular and not religious, it is not intent on fusional participation, but requires critical distance - the only thing that can guarantee the understanding of history. How could the community rite of fusion contribute to the historical liberation process? Ebrahim Hussein knows the fissional ceremonies and their illusions. He appreciates the epic, critical Ngugi of the first plays, the author whose work appealed to a spectator wanting to understand the world and the meaning of history, but he distances himself from the mystical, populist vein of the *Gikuyu* plays.

Ebrahim Hussein produced reflections on drama which received great response in Tanzania. He was one of the first to question the origins of theatre in Swahili, and went on to collect all the elements regarding the question of East African theatre. He did not separate this reflection from writing-practice, or even from performance. The essence of his reflection is found in his thesis written in English for the Humboldt University and in articles written since the sixties in English. At a conference on the meta-languages of literary studies, Ebrahim Hussein published a study on Aristotle (1980, translated in 1991), thus picking up the thread of his beginnings in drama theory.

Throughout the seventies a slow, continuous movement of literary and drama criticism accompanied the development of Swahili literature and the movement concentrated on the study of Ebrahim Hussein's works. He was one of the first to write a thesis on drama; he was a university professor, and his works were often prescribed for final year secondary school examinations. They have become classics. Julius Nyerere had translated Shakespeare; the school programme had to be completed with an original Swahili dramatist.

In what way was our professor, theorist and author read during the seventies? Most of the studies on his oeuvre were produced by academics associated with the teaching of Kiswahili; colleagues close to him. The intellectual milieu was narrow and campaigned for the cause of the development of Swahili language and literature studies.

Now that I have drawn the intellectual portrait of Ebrahim Hussein through his attempt to theorise on the birth and place of drama in Swahili literature, the time has come to study the production of the oeuvre which emerges from the Kenyan and Tanzanian criticism expressed in Kiswahili. I am merely reproducing here my reaction on first reading the oeuvre. This production of the oeuvre was revealed to me during my daily Kiswahili lessons from Professor Abdulaziz's Masters students, whom I had hired during my Nairobi sojourn from 1989 to 1991 as tutors, and whom I relentlessly invited to speak to me about the oeuvre of Ebrahim Hussein, their Ebrahim Hussein.

A militant Ebrahim emerged from their comments; one who was far from resembling the disillusioned man I had met a few years previously on a pavement in front of Dar es Salaam University, when he had told me that his salary hardly enabled him to take a taxi from his home to the office. That was in 1984, and again in 1988. That Ebrahim had resigned from his post; he had stated clearly why life had become impossible for him in his role as professor. He may have been the Ebrahim of the last plays, the one my student interlocutors did not read, or said they didn't understand.

It was clear that their Ebrahim was not mine. I wanted to know in greater detail who theirs was, the one they would communicate afterwards to their future pupils, and who had been taught for twenty years. This is the object of my next chapter.

3
Readings: History...

Ebrahim Hussein's reflections on drama are those of a theorist who is also a practitioner, an author and comedian. Widely read in his country during the seventies, he has been little performed since. His oeuvre is circulated, there are manuals to study it with, but it is rarely reviewed as a whole. The first thesis which was wholly devoted to him, that of Robert Philipson, *Drama and National Culture: a Marxist Study of Ebrahim Hussein* (Madison, 1989) is hampered by its Marxist orientation. The study, which is meant to be political and theoretical, too often misses the oeuvre's dramatic and lyrical movement, neglecting to consider it in its literary context or locate within the Tanzanian society of the mid-seventies and eighties, and the movement away from radical discourse and practice.

As the thesis abstract reads: "the Marxist framework was chosen in part for its harmony with the assumptions of local literary criticism. As a society which bills itself as in transition to socialism, Tanzania has fostered an intellectual tradition of radical discourse". What should be problematised is the contradiction between this discourse and Hussein's theoretical assumptions. This is precisely what the thesis prevents itself from doing in using a Marxist perspective. What's more, and it's a feeling I had ample occasion to confirm among Kiswahili students and lecturers who know Ebrahim Hussein's work well, quite often their reading froze the oeuvre: reifying it as a product of literary discussion, a goldmine of examination subjects, but in no way a living work, read in its entirety.

Swahili criticism of these plays is important because it is relayed by teaching, and produces the oeuvre's social image. Let's say it from the outset: this social image, this academic representation, is the one Ebrahim Hussein objects to, against which he is making an effort. He, contrary to me, thinks of it as desperately autonomisational. I think his effort is not futile; it's arduous, demanding, but it shows the fertile future of Swahili writing.

I'm conscious of the limits to what I am saying. Sengo's criticism, for example, represents the legitimate current of Swahili criticism found at the university. It is different from the open reading of Topan, who restricts himself to the early texts, which were published for East Africa by Oxford University Press. The essence of the critical texts concerns the first four plays, which are often exam material. In this chapter I will concentrate on these. They are the most published, the best known and the most widely reviewed. I will give a summary of them, followed by a brief commentary, before quoting the interpretations of the main Swahili critics. It provides a representation of Ebrahim Hussein's oeuvre, and the role that the writer is supposed to play within Tanzanian society, which coincides with other visions of socialist societies the world over. The problem is not limited to a reflection on Tanzanian socialism.

The artist's place in society via the autonomy of creation is at stake, a notion which is particularly delicate to handle in the case of men of the theatre, whose oeuvre must have a public, urban, political diffusion in order to exist. As I have indicated, language is the engine of national construction, which must be carried out in the name of socialism. A master of the language thus finds himself in a very uncomfortable, exposed position. We shall see in the following chapter on Swahili identity the means by which Hussein tries to express this discomfort. In the meantime, he probably thinks that ideologists and language teachers take far too much notice of him.

The first two plays, published in 1970, but which had been staged beforehand, particularly *Wakati Ukuta*, established Ebrahim Hussein's fame and showed his mastery. The characters from the plays have become types, representatives of Tanzanian youth from the first decade of independence. *Wakati Ukuta* (Time is a Wall) must be put into the context of sixties Dar es Salaam. School theatre, that of final year pupils, was already student theatre. A festival was organised at the Aga Khan School. Plays in Kiswahili were staged from this time onwards. The dramatic art Hussein calls Victorian, or which, following Brecht, we can call naturalist, contains all the conventions of nineteenth century 'bourgeois' theatre: picture-frame setting, linear construction, characters representing social types. Ebrahim's first two plays don't change them in any way.

Wakati Ukuta (Time is a Wall)

Wakati Ukuta - the title comes from a Swahili proverb: time is a wall against which we can only bang our heads - tells of the quarrel between Tatu and her parents who are annoyed when she goes to the cinema one evening with her boyfriend. They forbid her to go out. Tatu loses her temper and leaves the house to move in with Swai, a university dropout, whom she marries shortly afterwards. The parents regret having been so unyielding, and let Tatu know, through a female friend, that they forgive her. Finally, Tatu understands that Swai is not the boy she would like to live her life with; soon after their marriage he starts cheating on her. She leaves Swai and returns to her parents.

All's well that ends well: and yet, the play is not limited to the justification of a conventional social morality. Tatu and Swai really are types - sixties youngsters. Tatu's parents are enlightened bourgeois from Kariakoo, Dar es Salaam's Swahili quarter. The presentation of the characters is absolutely enlightening: no other play offers us such a luxury of details in the stage directions.

Tatu: 21 years old, wears a miniskirt, quite pretty, is a modern girl. Nature: gentle, not insolent.

Her father: Juma, 40-50 years old, kanzu, skull cap and trousers. No education, but wise. From the coast.

Her mother: Asha, 40-41 years old, baibui and veil, not really nasty at heart, despite appearances. Her fault: wanting her daughter to resemble her (if the reader considers that to be a fault). Full of energy. (For many people from the old order energy is a code with them)

Her girl friend: Kristina, 20 years old and modern, but the years have taught her very little, therefore her progress as far as clothes are concerned has not attained Tatu's level; she wears a Kanzu, but with decency. Modesty is a thing of the past for youngsters. Sweet tempered.

Her boy friend: Swai, 19-20 years old, a modern boy with avant-garde ideas; highly developed dress sense, but had to repeat his final school year. Stove-pipe trousers with frayed edges. Not a bad guy, but, as with many of today's boys, thinking does not come naturally.

Swai's girlfriend: 15-18 years old. Very pretty. God gave her everything, including the husbands of her girl friends. Is it her fault that men are mad about her?

Women 1,2,3: 43-50, full of compassion for their neighbours. When something happens in the neighbourhood, they come running to console the heart of whoever has been hit by misfortune. Helping one's neighbour means spreading the news everywhere, that's their one occupation.

Tatu's father understands that a change is needed, and that the children must be given greater liberty. He undertakes to convince his wife, who is more than ready to accept. The generation gap is the first of the possible readings which can be given to this play.

Kuna akina Tatu na Swai wengi siku hizi. Hawa wanawakilisha vijana wanaopenda kuiga mitindo mipya ya kisiku-hizi kama vile mavazi, kwenda densi, kuvaa nguo fupi, nk ... (Sengo, 1976:18)

There are many Tatu's and Swai's; they represent young people who like to copy today's new lifestyles by their dress, outings to nightclubs, miniskirts etc...

It also pits Tatu and her family against a boy who believes that marriage is a matter which can be resolved between young people only. Swai marries Tatu without their family's involvement. This type of behaviour would be that of someone who is not from the coast and who is thus not a Swahili Muslim.

Swai, kama angekuwa mzaliwa wa jamii hii hapana shaka asingefanya alivyofanya. Mazingira ya mchezo huu ni ya kipwani. Si pwani yote, bali miji ya pwoni, ni miji kama Dar es Salaam (Sengo, 1976:9).

If Swai had been born into this society, there is no doubt that he would not have done what he did. The background of this play is that of the coast, not the whole coast, but a coastal city, a city like Dar es Salaam.

Swai comes from the mountains, that is to say from the interior. He does not have Swahili manners or urbanity, and believes that a girl is to be had without much ado. Swai is not a Muslim, and many of the errors of his conduct could be linked to this fact. Hussein does not say that, but T. Sengo writes it:

> *Pengine kungetolewa wazo kwamba Wakati Ukuta ni mchezo uonyeshao uwezekano wa Mkristo na Mwislamu... Mkristo ampendaye Mwislamu ama watu wawili hawa wapendanapo wanapaswa kuzielewa thiolojia za dini zao. Chanzo na uzito wa mapenzi yao. Je dini zao zinawaruhusu? Watakapooana wataishi vipi?* (Sengo, 1976:11).

Maybe one can say that this play shows the relationships between Christians and Muslims. A Christian loves a Muslim girl: as always, when two people love one another, they must understand the theology of their religion. In what ways are the source and importance of their love involved? How will they live when they get married?

The dynamics of exchanges and clashes fit into the lake-mountain-coast framework, the first elements of which can be seen here. Coast culture is opposed to mountain culture, the *mlima*, in the same way that mountain culture will be opposed to lake culture in the last play. Here we find the first signs of that ecological vision of culture which is so strong in Ruganda's and so important to Hussein. T.S. Sengo prefers this interpretation grid which allows him to introduce the religious dimension. It is accompanied by a didactic tone, illustrating the importance of the critic in the constitution of a canonical corpus of contemporary, written Swahili literature, the new Tanzanian state's essential educational undertaking.

> *Hussein angepaswa kutueleza kwa kirefu juu ya ukweli wa ndoa za kinyumbani zifuatazo mila na desturi zetu; pia angetuonyesha kila kipengele cha maana ili tuweze kupima tofauti iliyopo kati ya ndoa hizo na hizi za akina Tatu* (Sengo, 1976:12).

Hussein should have explained to us the reality of local marriages, according to our own customs; and he should indicate to us every shade of meaning so that we can measure the difference between this type of marriage and that of Tatu.

The success of this play also comes from its moderation, and its call for lucidity. The author does not systematically take the youngsters' part, he tries to understand the parents and, finally - without saying it openly - he agrees with them. Young people shouldn't go too far too fast. Such was also the message of Wole Soyinka's first play, *The Lion and the Jewel*, staged and published in Nigeria in 1963. The artist poses as a teacher, as a mentor of the young generations; but he is almost the same age as his readers.

But, wanting to break down the wall of time is futile. For all that, should one submit oneself and accept the tyranny of parents adhering to a fixed vision of tradition? No, the young Ebrahim tells us, showing a great deal of maturity: one must be lucid, and intelligent parents will understand.

Tatu comes home. Is it the triumph of tradition? Not quite, for although she understands that she hasn't followed the straight and narrow, she has no intention of modifying her behaviour, and her parents have also understood that their anger was absurd. In *The Lion and the Jewel*, the young teacher thinks he has charmed the village beauty by his smooth talking. Yet, Sidi prefers the old, polygamous chief. Tradition is ingrained - and has an easy time of it - when compared to, in this case, an argumentative and idiotic, not to say fickle, modernity. Swai's modernity is empty-headed and gives nothing to the young girl it intends seducing, once the first few moments have passed. The young ladies' sense of liberty makes them reject these inept youngsters.

The sixties taught young girls to be wary of a new category of seducers arrayed with modernity's glamour. The message of Lawino, the heroine of *The Song of Lawino* by Okot p'Bitek (1966), is pertinent: the village beauty refuses to become a victim of the new politician. In Hussein's play Swai is an insignificant character without the social stature of Ocol, Lawino's husband, who is an intellectual and politician. However, the meaning of his failure is the same: the young woman is lucid, and Hussein is on her side.

Swahili literary criticism begins with the criticsm of Hussein's plays. Balisidiya taught didactics of literature in a teachers' training college before being recognised as a novelist and a critic (1975). She uses *Wakati Ukuta* to illustrate her method of textual commentary. This illustrates the importance of these works which shape the sensitivity, as well as the intellectual discipline, of the pupils and students. Balisidya divides the characters into three groups: neighbourhood women, youngsters and Tatu's father.

Public opinion, "what will people say?" is a great source of inertia which only Tatu's father escapes from. Balisidya sees a contradiction between Tatu's desire for freedom and her blindness in becoming besotted with Swai, who neither promises nor gives anything worthwhile. In Swahili literary pedagogics, which she is conscious of creating, the analysis of oral literature is a means of attaining a critical conscience. Like a good pedagogue she relies on the intellectual resources of her pupils, and considers that oral literature must be one of them.

She summarises the play in four proverbs: *saburi yavuta heri*, patience brings happiness; *wapiganapo tembo, nyasi zinaumia*, when elephants fight, the grass suffers; *hasira ya mkizi, furaha ya mvuvi*, the squid's anger is the fisherman's pleasure; *haraka haraka haina baraka*, haste is a bad counsellor. Two of the proverbs are in praise of patience and two apply to lucidity. Her moral discussion of these texts is also a call for inner lucidity which concerns all of us: the conflict is situated between the person and his actions (Balisidya, 1975:14-15).

The writer is read like a teacher of ethics, for the use of pupils and students, by both Sengo and Balisidya. When it comes to a man of the theatre, there is nothing original in this approach. The oeuvre's different readings complement one another. The author calls on the youngsters to be lucid. He turns the young Muslim girl into a lucid character, and the young Christian into someone irresponsible. The eruption of continentals into the life of the coastal inhabitants caused break-offs the author doesn't complain about, but which he chronicles, whilst subtly indicating ways to go beyond them. The world changes: it does not collapse.

The other play staged during the same period, *Alikiona* is a farce with three characters, consisting of three scenes. It is the story of a cuckold husband with a praiseworthy sense of balance, after the turpitudes of the previous plays' male hero.

Alikiona (She saw that which ...)

Saãda makes her husband Omar believe she has gone to spend the weekend with her mother while she is, in fact, with her lover Abdallah. At the same time, her mother passes away. Saãda is unaware of this event but her husband is aware. When, upon her return, Saãda brings her husband a gift supposed to come from his mother-in-law, the duplicity of her conduct is suddenly revealed. Saãda can do little more than cry while begging her husband to hit her, which he does not do.

Ebrahim Hussein shows his mastery in the mechanics of intrigue, typical of the *kichekesho*. His clarity of construction, vivacity of language and succinctness of wording, are united in a rather sombre poetic vision of relations between the sexes. On the position of the cuckold husband, Hussein constructs an intrigue which is remarkably simple and efficient. The title alludes to a Swahili proverb: "*Alikiona cha mtema kuni*": she suffered what the woodcutter's head suffered! In other words, the unfaithful wife deserves what she gets!

In the first reference volume on Swahili literature, published by Oxford University Press, Sengo titles his analysis: "Mere meanness or bestiality?". His argument is that the wife behaves like an animal in this play, insulting her husband and failing in all her family duties by not going to her mother's burial. Can she be excused by the suggestion that her husband is impotent? There is nothing indicating this state in the husband, and certainly not the insults she directs at him in her fury.

> *Ama angempiga, au angempa talaka. Lakini nafikiri Omari anatuonyesha katika vitendo vyake kwamba anachukulia kuwa wanawake ni sawa na watoto wadogo ... Naona Omari ni mtu mwenye busara, hekima, subira na akili ... (Sengo, 1976:10)*

Either he must hit her, or he must divorce her. But Omar shows us by his actions that he treats women like children. Omar is full of wisdom, patience and discernment.

Sengo lacks a sense of nuance and his criticism of vaudeville is a violent charge against the position of women in the new Tanzanian society, notably against their freedom of movement. The play's mechanism is formidably efficient and leaves no room for the creation of subtle characters as in the previous play. The flood of big words to which Sengo subjects us in this *kichekesho*, this comic interlude which would have pleased *taarab* spectators, misses its target or, rather, misleads its target. Ebrahim Hussein continues a recognized genre, using tried recipes: a lover hidden in the room the husband enters, a female liar exposed by coincidence. Nevertheless, he leaves the play open ended: we don't know how the relations between Omar and Saāda will develop. She insults her husband by calling him *khanithi* (effeminate, or impotent, according to Sacleux).

The punishment Saāda calls for is already a type of penance and has nothing to do with the *bestiality* - the term *unyama* is very strong in Kiswahili with which Sengo overwhelms her. Saāda's behaviour is reprehensible, but pardon is also a dimension of human relationships. To crush Saāda under the ignominy of bestiality is to deny pardon, to deny a certain form of humanity.

Sengo is conscious of the excess of his words, since he concludes his article with a *Sura* from the Koran, which precisely opens the way to pardon. These plays already resist simplistic schemes and present critics with problems we will encounter again in the course of our analysis of the oeuvre. The prevailing critical attitude is akin to a didactic and moralising vision of literature which Ebrahim Hussein does not share.

Udhaifu mkubwa katika tamthilia hizi mbili ni kwamba mwandishi haelezi mgongano wa kitamaduni na upotofu wa maadili na amali za kijamii unatokana na mfumo gani unayosababisha. (Mutegi, 1985:59)

The great weakness of these two plays is that the writer doesn't explain to us which concept of life the cultural conflict and the corruption stem from. Good literature explains the actions and the nature of the world which caused them.

Ebrahim's problem is probably that he fundamentally disagrees with this definition: he is not alone. From the first plays onwards the main traits of Tanzanian criticism were put in place; the university is the strategic centre of cultural as well as political legitimacy. Tanzanian culture is produced through the creation, in Kiswahili, of a theatrical, poetic and theoretical nature, and especially thanks to it; this creation is discussed, evaluated and then diffused through researchers and critics assembled at university and in authorities of production and evaluation of Tanzanian literature. We always find the same names in journals, in papers, in collections of articles, in prefaces and probably in examination committees.

These university critics were still active in 1995. Sengo, who we keep coming back to, was director of the Institute for Research in Kiswahili and he still plays a role in the Tanzanian intelligentsia. The undertaking to constitute a pool of common references in the same language is systematically driven, and finds a choice terrain in Hussein's work. All the more because, after the first two plays which dealt with family life and domestic conflicts, our author tackles historical theatre with *Kinjeketile*.

The play, which was performed and published in 1969, was written when the author started his university career in Dar es Salaam. In that year's university brochure, Hussein's name appears as a member of the drama department, and his research subject deals with school theatre. Professor Feibach, whom we've cited for his work on Brecht, staged *Kinjeketile*, his young colleague's play. A few years later he supervised Hussein's doctoral thesis at the Humboldt University in East Berlin, where he still lectures today - an eminent specialist of contemporary theatre. *Kinjeketile*, staged at the university theatre in 1969, precedes Seydou Badian's *Chaka's Death* (1963), staged in January 1970.

Kinjeketile (the hero's name)

The play consists of four acts *(sehemu)* divided into tableaux *(onyesho)*. In the first act set in the village of Kinjeketile, the chief soothsayer to whom the spirits promised that water would bring invincibility; the foreman enters in the third tableau for an illlustration of the colonialists' power, and to represent exploitation. The second act is very long (25 of the 50 pages); we are still in Kinjeketile's village and await the result of the conversations with the spirits. The crowd urges Kinjeketile to give the revolt signal, but he cannot make up his mind to do so.

In the third act Kitunda plays the role of the narrator in epic theatre and tells us of the battle in which the *Maji Maji* fighters are defeated; water has not made them invulnerable and the lesson they learn is a cruel one. Finally, the fourth act is set in the prison camp. This act contains only one tableau: Kinjeketile analyses with lucidity and bitterness what happened, but refuses to deny the magic water's power, despite the pressure of his jailers.

Kinjeketile shows the influence of Brechtian theories efficiently handled by the young author, on epic theatre. Only, Hussein was not about to let himself be enrolled so easily and to become Tanzania's official playwright. The epic hero, Kinjeketile, understands the desperate situation and provides us with the elements of his understanding. All in all, he's a tragic hero, which is not part of the epic theatre programme, as defined by Brecht, and which the construction and conclusion of this play would have us believe. The hero doubts, he is an ambiguous prophet, not really a war chief. The play is based on historical research of the birth of Tanzanian nationalism. A new state, anxious to build a nation according to socialist principles, needs epic theatre: that is to say, it needs to portray positive heroes whose example stimulates young people. In his thesis, Hussein criticises the plays with historic subjects staged in Dar es Salaam, and wonders what type of hero to put on stage. A character like Martin Kayamba, the prototype of the new African, founder of the union movement in Tanganyika, was too much a prisoner of European culture-models to constitute a figure likely to spark the enthusiasm of younger generations.

The *Maji Maji* revolt seems quite solid ground for a dramatised work. It produced historical works and took place close to a region Hussein knows well: somewhere on the Rufiji near Kilwa, where he was born, and Lindi, where the German headquarters were located.

Other nationalist figures, pioneers of the anticolonial struggle, like Mkwawa, had been the subject of plays, but it was difficult to separate their struggle from their tribal origin.

> The Maji Maji movement was important in three ways. Firstly it was a new way to try and regain independence. Tribal resistance had failed because it had not been united. The Maji Maji movement tried to reunite people without bothering about their origins. Religion was used for this. Every combatant drank water; normally he was sprinkled with it. It protected him from the bullets and committed him to the war and to fraternity. At first the water was distributed by the priests of Kolelo, a spirit living in the mountains of Uluguru. Later it was linked to the belief that a new world would come, a world without evil, governed by a new god. He would change the world and it would become a new world. His reign would be a reign of wonders. Maji Maji was different from tribal resistance. The Germans called it a people's revolt. Yet Maji Maji failed either to regain independence or to preserve the unity in which it had begun. A mass movement needs strong organisation, and the religious organisation of Maji Maji was not strong enough. As German millitary pressure increased, the movement disintegrated into tribal sections. When the Ngoni joined, for example, they fought alone, and were defeated alone (Cliffe, 1975:9-10).

This play put Hussein in the vanguard of East African theatre, bringing to the Tanzanian stage an historical and patriotic oeuvre which had previously been lacking but which went on to represent Tanzanian theatre for many years. For example, in Lagos in 1977, at the *Second World Black and African Festival of Arts and Culture*, Tanzania staged *Kinjeketile*. It is worth noting that at the same festival Wole Soyinka's resolution recommending the adoption of Kiswahili as the Pan-African language was adopted. Hussein, who was in Lagos with his play, did not have the opportunity to meet the future Nobel prize-winner in an official capacity and seemed to regret it twenty years later.

Kinjeketile had been translated into English by the author himself a few years previously. The only one of Ebrahim Hussein's eight plays to be published in English, it was read by critics who knew no

Kiswahili. It is thus a part of the repertoire of historical African theatre, precisely because it was translated. Numerous historical plays on the heroes of the resistance or the wars waged by African kings against colonial powers, were published in the sixties. *Chaka's Death* (1963) is one of the first, and one of the best known, which is curious, because Chaka did not fight the colonising Whites who viewed his undertaking to destroy the neighbouring clans with interest. He became the symbol of the African sovereign and the tragedy of power. Chaka dies, murdered by his brothers, and prophesies the coming of the Whites with his dying breath; Kinjeketile chooses to die in order to keep the faith of his followers intact.

In *Albouri's Exile* (1967), Albouri takes refuge in the interior of the country. In *Kondo, the Shark* (1965) the character of the Dahomean King Béhanzin, who waged a real war against France, is a fighter without Kinjeketile's qualms. This epic theatre, this instrument of national construction, was mocked by Wole Soyinka in one of his first plays, *A Dance of the Forests* (1963), in which the African king is a corrupt slaver and certainly not a freedom-fighter. English critics would turn Kinjeketile into an example of *"realist, socialist, historic"* tragic drama as opposed to *"individualist and bourgeois"* tragedy, that of Wole Soyinka in *Death and the King's Horseman*.

Biodun Jeyifo (an excellent critic and probably the best interpreter of Soyinka's oeuvre) seems to be misled by a partial vision of this Swahili work shown in Lagos almost a decade after its first production. For him, in *Kinjeketile*, "the archetype of tragic action and socio-cultural milieu, are probed within the framework of truly historical circumstances and confrontations. And the confrontation is not between lonely individuals and society but between individuals and forces which embody the irreconcilable goals and aspirations of social groups and classes or competing nations and alliances" (Jeyifo, 1985: 42). Even though he finds Kinjeketile a "Hamlet - like character", he tends to underplay the reluctance of the hero to become a true political leader. Thus the historical tragedy Kinjeketile is put at the same level as Ngugi and Mugo's *The Trial of Dedan Kimathi* (1976).

The example of Aimé Césaire is also quoted, especially *A Season in the Congo* (1966), which is a politically committed play against the imperialist forces which shot Lumumba. And yet the appropriate reference is probably Aimé Césaire's *The Tragedy of King Christophe* (1963), whose central character is indeed the tragic hero of an epic play, a king, a head of his people. Kinjeketile is also a head due to the powers his trance bestows on him.

The analysis of *Kinjeketile* is classic work of Swahili criticism in Kenya and Tanzania. The work has often been prescribed for examinations, and all high school pupils know it. From the first studies a contradiction is detected between the character and history, between Kinjeketile and the *Maji Maji* revolt. This contradiction is not dealt with in detail and, eventually, moves to a secondary level, eclipsed by the movement of history. Jay Kitsao states it clearly in his essay: "the most important character of the play is perhaps Kitunda". The author, professor at the University of Nairobi, a noted scholar and a playwright himself, has the merit of trying to elucidate Kinjeketile's behaviour with care. He has devoted a lengthy study to the characters and, very clearly, distinguishes between the possessed Kinjeketile and the normal Kinjeketile.

For Jay Kitsao, the play's eponymous hero has several faces and the historical Kinjeketile, who can be found in the German archives and in oral tradition, should be spared a thought. This historical Kinjeketile does not interest Hussein at all, as he took pains to tell us in the preface to his play. In Jay Kitsao's study, the possessed Kinjeketile is a sort of messiah, a prophet of unity, going beyond tribal conflicts. The critic establishes a parallel between Kinjeketile's action and that of Jesus:

> *Water is a form of baptism, the spirit which owns it is also a form of Holy Spirit; and, as for the word, it will become action. The discourse of unity is applauded, and Kinjeketile sends his listeners on a mission:* "Nendeni kama upepo, kusini, kaskazini, magharibi" ("Go like the wind, to the south, to the north, to the west") (Kitsao, 1977: 2).

This assimilation with Jesus is based on Kinjeketile's messianism, and his inspired words. However, the liberation promised by Jesus, which differs from that of Moses, is not political liberation. We find it rather superficial developing this analogy when there exists a substantial difference in objective. Kitsao sticks to this comparison and strengthens it by trying to catch our author red-handed in self-contradiction in an essay on Mohammed Said Abdullah's detective novels (Hussein, in Topan, 1971).

For Hussein these texts, featuring a Black Sherlock Holmes in Zanzibar are artificial. London is not Zanzibar; and it is not enough to change the name and the colour of the hero. But that is exactly what Hussein does, according to Kitsao who is apparently very eager to follow up the comparison. Kinjeketile is a Black Jesus - why blame Mohammed Said Abdullah's detective for being a Black Sherlock Holmes?

Onyesho la Kinjeketile limetawaliwa na kujengwa juu ya mambo aliyoyafanya Yesu katika Biblia. Yaonekana kwamba yeye vilevile kabadilisha jina la Yesu na jina la mahali... akambadilisha rangi na kumweka Tanganyika... Akamfanya Mmatumbi. (Kitsao, 1977:28)

Kinjeketile's vision has been directed and constructed from Jesus's actions in the Bible; it seems that Hussein only changed the place-name. Instead of Jesus, he wrote 'Kinjeketile', he changed his colour, put him in Tanganyika and made a Black Man out of him.

Later on Kitsao offers the following admonition:

Ebrahim Hussein anaifanya historia kuwa kipimo cha kazi ya mwenzake lakini hataki kazi yake mwenyewe itolewe makosa kwa kutofuata historia (Kitsao, 1977: 29)

Ebrahim Hussein turns history into the measure of his colleague's oeuvre, but doesn't want his oeuvre to be judged in relation to history.

We have trouble following this rather specious reasoning, which smacks of a settling of scores between colleagues. But, it makes up the greater part of the first detailed criticism of Kinjeketile illustrating one of the most regrettable aspects of the small number of critics working on Swahili literature during the seventies: a confusion between genres, a mixture of scientific arguments and clan quarrels.

Why does Kitsao defend his colleague in this way? Why is this polemic in a study meant to be a source of reference for students? The number of tribunes available to Swahili critics is probably limited, and Kitsao did not want to miss this opportunity. The general themes of his criticism are well summarised in a later work:

> *Aina ya kwanza ni maudhui ya vita vya ukombozi dhidi ya ukoloni mkongwe. Haya ndiyo maudhui makuu Hussein anayojadili katika Kinjeketile. Lengo la mkoloni lilikuwa ni kuimarisha uchumi wake kwa kuinyonya nchi ya Tanganyika. Anatudokeza pia matatizo yaliyotokea ya uongozi na kusababisha kushindwa kwa Watanganyika na majeshi ya Kijerumani. Tamthilia hii hali kadhalika inatueleza kwamba kiongozi wa vita hivi, Kinjeketile, alitumia maji, siyo kuwazurua Watanganyika, bali kuwaunganisha. Jinsi mwandishi anavyoeleza vita vya Maji Maji kwa uhalisi unaozingatia ukweli wa kihistoria kunaipa tamthilia hii sifa ya fasihi yakinifu ...* (Mutegi, 1985: 158)

The first of the themes is the battle between the forces of liberation and colonialism. It is the essential theme of what is presented to us in Kinjeketile. The aim of the colonialists was to strengthen their economy by exploiting Tanganyika. He reveals to us problems linked to management which caused the Tanganyikans defeat by the Germans. This play explains to us that the leader of this battle, Kinjeketile, used water not to stir up the Tanganyikans but to unite them. The way the writer realistically explains the war to us considers history's truth and allows us to give this play the merit of realism.

The pan-ethnic nature of the *Maji Maji* movement, and the concern not to act in the name of a single earthly god, but to show the unity of the traditional gods, are very important. Ebrahim Hussein does not criticise the religion of the Tanzanian people; on the contrary, he shows that it can be a unifying factor and that the sign of this unity is water. For him, true to Brechtian theory, the theatre is the place where history offers itself to be understood: the spirits of the *WaRufiji* and of the *WaZaramo* are the same; Kolelo is the brother of the god of the *WaRufiji*, Hongo, who possesses Kinjeketile.

The supra-tribal unity, observed by the Germans who turned the movement into a people's revolt, is also the moment of a linguistic invention, that of standard Kiswahili, which here becomes the object of a sort of *glossolalia*. Kinjeketile is inspired when he speaks the language, and religion helps to understand the ferments of the popular unity. In the following chapter we will come back to the inventions of the possessed Kinjeketile, whose trance seems to constitute a sort of blind spot in the work, a place where Kiswahili is spoken, from where Arabs will take power and will replace colonialists. Kitsao breathes no word about these themes but, on the contrary, tackles the other characters in detail. He does show us that Kinjeketile is not a coward but, in his moments of lucidity, a clearsighted chief who doesn't want to send his troops to be butchered. The history of the anti-colonial struggle expected another type of behaviour from him; it is, therefore, necessary to make an extensive study of the other characters. Kitunda, Kinjeketile's main interlocutor, is courageous, sometimes quick-tempered, but always loyal:

> *Swali likiulizwa, ni nani mhusika mtawala hadithi katika mchezo wa Kinjeketile itabidi kuchagua baina ya Kinjeketile, na Kitunda. Bila shaka, Ebrahim Hussein aliazimia kumfanya Kinjeketile mtawala hadithi... Lakini tukimfikiria yule anayeshiriki zaidi katika mambo yanayoendelea mchezoni, bila shaka tutamchagua Kitunda* (Kitsao, 1977: 36).

If we ask ourselves who is the play's main character, we have to choose between Kinjeketile and Kitunda. Hussein would probably have declared that it was Kinjeketile. However, if we ask ourselves who has the largest role in the play's action, we will choose Kitunda.

Kitunda wants to fight, but on equal terms, and only when it is too late does he realize the weakness of his own troops. He believes in the virtues of water - until he sees that it protects no-one. He knows how important training is for soldiers. Although superstitious in the beginning, in action he nevertheless shows himself to be a positive spirit. He organises the army into regiments. He is, thus, a truly positive character. Kitsao also examines the role of the female characters. After Tatu, the modern young girl, and the bestial Saada, we have here two model wives who know their place "according to African custom":

> *Hata wakati akiongea na watu wengine nyumbani kwake, mkewe hatakikani karibu. Kinjeketile anawaingiza watu ndani ya nyumba yake na kuzungumza nao kwa faragha ...* (Kitsao, 1977: 41).

> *When he speaks to other people in his house, his wife should keep far away from them. He lets his guests into the house to speak to them secretly.*

For Sarah Mirzah, who reflects upon the lessons of this play in another article within the same collective volume, the strength of Hussein's oeuvre comes from his description of the preparation for war, of the work of popular unrest led by rumour, and of the process of becoming conscious, achieved by Kinjeketile's messianic speech, to which should be added Kitunda's talent as an organiser and the impetuousness of a third character, Ngulumbalyo. She sees the entire play in the light of the epic combat:

> *Kosa la Kinjeketile - ikiwa hilo kweli ni kosa - katika uongozi wake pia ni funzo. Kiongozi kamwe hawezi kuongoza watu wake kwa imani imara ikiwa yeye mwenyewe haamini atamkayo, au hajiamini yeye mwenyewe binafsi ... Ebrahim Hussein ...ametuwezesha kuhisi zaidi mambo hayo yaliyotokea nchini Tanganyika kuliko angelikuwa ameyaandika katika kitabu cha historia ...* (Mirzah, 1977: 4)

Kinjeketile's mistake, if it can be called one, has a lesson in it: that the chief cannot advance the struggle if he doesn't believe in what he says, or if he doesn't have confidence in himself. Hussein enables us to understand what happened in Tanganyika better than if he had written a history book.

Like Balisidya, Mirzah, a pedagogue of Swahili language and literature, is pleased about Hussein's success - which provides new quality texts for pupils, and widens the space of the ideas debate in Kiswahili. However, she criticises the way Hussein handled the struggle itself, and deplores the fact that the war is neither shown nor described. From an epic point of view, it is clear that combat strategy is not analysed, and that the conflict episodes do not interest the author very much. This point, taken up by Kitsao, seems to be the object of a certain consensus. The play's theme is probably not the struggle of nations but, rather, the doubts of the leader. Kitsao himself brings some elements to this line of thought when he finds that the German strategy is not credible:

Angemfanya Mjerumani kupeleka vikosi vya askari mara moja na kuwashambulia watu kabla hawa jaungana na siyo kujiketia tu akingojea. Sidhani kama utawala wowote wa kawaida ungefanya namna alivyofanya Mjerumani katika mchezo wa Hussein. (Kitsao, 1977:41)

He should have had the Germans send in their troops to attack the people before they united – rather than just sitting there and waiting. I don't think that any normal government would have done what the Germans did in Hussein's play.

Once defeat has been inflicted, Kinjeketile refuses to accede to the demands of the Germans, who would want to see him condemn revolt and superstition. The epic hero believes in the virtues of illusion in politics, and yet, his indecision was partially responsible for his defeat.

The central theme of the critics' comments concerns the history of national construction. There is a separation between the main character, Kinjeketile, and the movement he has started. The embarrassment caused by his erratic behaviour is expressed by the strange comparison with Jesus. Kitsao also evokes Hussein's first poem, *Ngoma na Vailini* (Abdulaziz, 1979:105), in which the author hesitated between the cross and the Swahili *kanzu*.

For our author, personal identity is intimately linked to religious identity. The figure of the doubting hero becomes a figure of Christ – a strange break from the theatre, whereas there is a character, as suggested by Biodun Jeyifo closer to Kinjeketile than Christ, namely Hamlet. However, the prince of Elsinore seems rather incongruous amid *Maji Maji* warriors; to risk a strange analogy, one would have difficulty in seeing Hamlet leading the *Mau Mau*. Ngugi and Mugo's

Dedan Kimathi is a sort of one-dimensional Che Guevara, while Kinjeketile fascinates by what he hides and can't express.

The final message, the refusal to give in to alienation, in a word, accepting death, is a sort of suicide evoking that of King Christophe (Césaire, 1963), a call to future generations. It gives a final, epic chord to a play which contains precious little which can be called that: its hero is too filled with the tragedy of history, lost and admired amidst an anti-colonial epic.

The critics we have already read produce a discourse on society and literature, and seem to reflect little on art, literature and their own means of expression in Kiswahili. *Kinjeketile* is praised for its description of the heroic struggle of a 'virtual' Tanzanian people against German colonialists in 1905. *Kinjeketile*'s own unique problems, the theory of power allows us to glimpse the sombre nature of his predictions - all of that is put aside and does not interest the critics.

The first two plays, *Alikiona* and *Wakati Ukuta*, have become classics of the school repertoire. The background against which they take place, their novel and efficient language, the conflicts of generations and of sexes which they deal with in a clear way - and their own kind of enlightened conservatism, ensure their success with pupils, students and critics.

The wall of time, necessary patience; these things were not on the agenda during the period after Independence. That patience would be Kinjeketile's message, once his people's unity had been achieved. The failure of those who don't listen to him also illustrates the error of wanting to get over this wall of time too quickly.

This message is still disconcerting, even though its epic dramaturgy is difficult for us to accept today.

4
Readings, politics...

In 1971, Ebrahim Hussein published *Mashetani*, which constitutes his most ambitious play. It's also the first text (and this will occupy us for quite some time) in which the divorce between Hussein and the Tanzanian critics becomes apparent. It would take six years for it to be staged at the university theatre. The previous works created types, and showed a hero; now the author wants to go further, and to understand the dreams and anguish of his countrymen. Yet the demons he lets loose, the *Mashetani* (in the singular- *shetani* - a word of Arab origin in which satan can be heard) are not acceptable to some of the Tanzanian critics who blame Hussein for his obscurity, and who pull away from him from this play onwards.

Mashetani

In Act 1, we are in front of the Baobab, the favourite tree of the evil spirits or demons. Juma plays a demon's game, and becomes one: Kitaru plays at becoming the representative of humanity - man. The demon plays with man, but man kills him after his wishes have been granted.

In Act 2, we are in Dar in Kitaru's posh house. The two students are talking, planning an evening at the cinema, then giving it up. Kitaru's father arrives in his brand-new Benz. Kitaru talks with his father about the demons. Shortly afterwards, a doctor arrives, summoned by Kitaru's parents who find the latter strange. The doctor declares that Kitaru is ill, and admits being powerless.

In Act 3 we are at Juma's house. His grandmother is nostalgic for the good old days of the plantations and feudalism, while Juma's mother works to keep the family alive. Juma is in a bar where he listens to the conversations of the patrons representing the new Tanzanian culture.

In Act 4, we're back at Kitaru's house. Juma has come to visit him. A new play on demons, which becomes a game of truth. An explanation takes place between the two friends and, finally, Juma leaves his friend, declaring that he who climbs a stairway can only meet in passing whoever is going down it. The author already quoted this sentence in his introduction. The whole play is a meditation on truth, on the meaning of our actions in a new political situation. The demon is the wind of doubt, but he is also truth.

From a dramaturgical point of view, this play is an important turning point in his oeuvre. It contains four parts: the first comprises twelve pages and a single scene; the second twenty-three pages and four scenes; the third, nine pages and two scenes; finally, the fourth comprises thirteen pages and two scenes. An entire part of the play, the second, is supposed to be dreamt by one of the characters. In other words, theatre must also take into account immaterial realities like dreams or anxiety.

> *Mashetani inahusu jinsi Mwafrika alivyorithi mfumo wa kibepari na athari zake zote, na jinsi hawezi kujiendeleza kwa sababu mfumo huu unatawaliwa na ukoloni mambo-leo. Katika tamthilia hii mwandishi anatufafanulia jinsi mfumo wa kitabaka ulioachwa na mkoloni unavyosababisha migogoro katika jamii za Kiafrika* (Mutegi, 1985:160).

Mashetani deals with the way in which the African inherited the capitalist mentality with all its signs, and the way in which this mentality, which puts him under the control of neo-colonialism, prevents development. In this play, he shows how the class mentality left by the colonialists caused conflicts in African society.

Mashetani is hailed as a work of great mastery, too complicated to be understood. From the start, it gave rise to a political reading as it portrayed students representing two different backgrounds: the former feudals and the new bureaucrats, the 'Wazungu Weusi', the 'Black Europeans' Nyerere spoke about (Mvungi: 1975:16).

Kinjeketile had doubts about a course of action, but continued the battle. Here the son of the Zanzibari-family, Juma, stops fighting – or, rather, no longer knows what to do when faced with the scepticism or even, sometimes, the cynicism which fills him. The only answer is theatre, the game through which he tries to catch the conscience of his interlocutor. Via the game the demons come on stage in order to give a face to what obscurely plagues society.

The form of epic theatre is well and truly exhausted, and Brecht is far away: decidedly, political reality is no longer of an epic order. Hussein has understood this hard but powerful message before many others. Political reality calls for other forms of figuration, closer to psychodrama, when facing the double inappropriateness of Victorian theatre (an outmoded colonial heritage) and epic theatre (an outrageous revolutionary dream). What is real here is what is acted: the game involving the demons and the bourgeois house in the dream. Political reality is made up of conflicts for which no charismatic leader has the solution; certainly a word is needed - but one which does not surpass his creator, and does not destroy him.

Kitaru: hata sielewi nianze wapi. Unasikia Juma ... Hebu tuanze ... Ninahisi nini nataka kusema, lakini akili haiupi ulimi maneno yanayoelezea kuhisi kwangu, au feelings zangu. Na akili, vile vile pengine haifahamu tatizo hili; lakini ninahisi. Kwa mfano, toka tumepata uhuru, sisi Waafrika hapa, imekuwa kama tumeingia ... ehe, mfano mzuri ... imekuwa kama tumeingia katika jahazi moja nzuri sana, na jina letu limeandikwa, lakini, nahodha... nahodha ni nani? (MA:21)

Kitaru: I don't even know where to start ... You see, Juma...Let us start...I feel what I want to say, but the brain does not give the tongue words which express my feelings (sic). And maybe even my brain does not understand this problem; but I feel, for example, since gaining our independence, we Africanshere, its as if we have entered...yes, a good example, its as if we had entered one very beautiful dhow, and our name was written, but the captain, who is the captain?

This play has not been translated into a European language, and only one review of it existed in English before the more detailed studies which appeared in the theses of Amandina Lihamba (1985) and Robert Philipson (1989). A review which appeared in the journal, *Kiswahili*, in 1978, after the play's première at the university theatre, deals with the stage direction, but gives a glimpse of a few essential elements of a canonical (that is to say Tanzanian and academic) reading of the work. For Ohly, the student production was a superficial reading insisting on the problem of *nouveaux riches* in socialist society, while the work's deeper structure deals with the possibility of controlling mystic forces.

Juma the Zanzibari would be the guardian of the last traditional forces, that which exist beyond rational tradition. Kitaru must live with the conviction that the university will allow him to acquire political skills and knowledge, while his father will teach him about business. That does not give him access to the essential powers of life - to traditional forces contained in the baobab.

> *Mashetani, as replayed by students, concerned not Hamlet, but court intrigues; not Kitaru, but 'petit bourgeois' conflicts - which is regrettable* (Ohly, 1978 :108).

The essential conflict would be mystical and not political. Swahili critics are very embarrassed by which interpretation to give. And yet, this is the play on which we have found the largest number of reviews, because it is very often prescribed for the final examinations, although it is considered difficult, or even too complicated. A quarter of a century later, it can be read as a surprising parable of class conflicts linked to the establishment of a new socialist society for which the author expresses profound scepticism, disguised as dramatic play.

> *Mwandishi anatumia fumbo la shetani na binadamu kuonyesha matatizo yanayokabili watu waliotawaliwa kwa muda mrefu* (Mvungi, 1975:20).

The writer uses the "riddle, game" parable of the demon and the man to show problems coming to the surface in people who were dominated for a long time.

All of that was not audible, or visible, in 1971, or even in 1977, unless Ohly's mystical interpretation heralds this political reassessment:

> *Katika mchezo wa Mashetani, Ebrahim Hussein anaonekana amekua zaidi. Mchezo wake Wakati Ukuta, ama Alikiona ni mchezo wa kusomwa na jamii yote, yeyote awezaye kusoma. Mchezo wa Kinjeketile umepunguza idadi ya wasomaji wake; Mashetani ndio mchezo uliopunguza zaidi idadi wa wasomaji wake*

(na hao ni wachache mno); hata miongoni mwa wasomi wa kiwango cha juu, ni wachache wanaoweza kukisoma na kukielewa mara ya kwanza (Mutegi, 1985: 21).

In *Mashetani*, Hussein shows that he has made a lot of progress. *Wakati Ukuta*, or *Alikiona* are plays that can be read by the whole of society. *Kinjeketile* reduced the number of his readers, *Mashetani* reduced them even more (and there are few); and even amongst readers on a high level some cannot read and understand him the first time.

The theme of political conscience is accentuated by all the critics:

Badala yake, viongozi walianzisha tabaka la "Wazungu weusi" ambalo lilianza kuwanyonya wananchi. Twaweza kuona jinsi athari ya kizungu ilivyowaingia Juma na Kitaru (Mvungi, 1976:18-19).

Our leaders shaped the class of black Europeans who began to exploit the people. We saw evidence of these Western ways in Juma and Kitaru.

The political reading gives an explanatory framework by opposing the aristocrats and the bureaucrats, Juma and Kitaru. There would thus be two classes: the former planters and the new rulers, the *"nomenklaturists"* enriched by commerce. This class opposition confirms an opposition between Zanzibar and the continent, which Hussein must be particularly sensitive to, as we shall see in the next chapter.

Juma, the historian, comes from a world which has disappeared. Kitaru the jurist, full of faith in the future, understands from a history book that Juma's lost world has left many scars. The critics insist, at every possible opportunity, on the responsibility of the colonialists in this state of affairs. The play is punctuated with the sardonic bursts of laughter of an invisible character who, to everyone, is obviously the colonialist, the keeper of a secret which enslaves the characters.

Vivyo hivyo, wakoloni walipotoa uhuru walitucheka kama vile wanajua tutashindwa kujiendesha. Kwa hiyo, muda wote tunapogongana wenyewe kwa sababu ya mfumo tuliorithi, wao wanatucheka kwa mbali (Mvungi, 1976:19).

The colonialists granted independence, but they laughed because they knew that we could not succeed in governing ourselves. So, every time we bungle up because of the structures we have inherited, they laugh at us from afar.

This secret would be Western-type 'education' which made African 'black Europeans', and which enables the colonialist to pursue his domination because it is now exerted insidiously on people's very minds. As Topan (1977) says, the drug which captured the minds of the Africans is *neocolonialism*. The former situation, the one Juma comes from, is over: what is happening to Juma and to his family may not be undeserved. Today, there is the danger of a new drug. The relationship between Juma and Kitaru, between the demon and the man, represents this new danger.

Uhusiano baina ya binadamu na shetani unakuwa uhusiano baina ya wazalendo na Mkoloni kwenye mazingira ya mbuyu: siasa. Mbuyu ni siasa; Shetani huwaingia watu mbuyuni, mkoloni huwaingia watu kisiasa. Wazalendo wanataka waungane, wawe kitu kimoja, wawe huru. Wanataka wapate uhuru kamili, uhuru kisiasa, uhuru kiuchumi, uhuru kiutamaduni. Mkoloni, shetani, hapendezwi na jambo hilo (Topan,1977: 51).

The relationship between man and the demon is the relationship between patriots and colonialists in the Baobab-context: that is to say, in politics. The demon possesses the men in the baobab. Colonialism takes possession of men through politics. The patriots want unity, political, economic and cultural freedom. The colonialist, the demon, does not want to hear talk of that.

The game between the man and the demon is an allegorical unveiling of history. The knife which the demon holds out to the man is certainly an instrument of power of the independent state - the monopoly of legitimate violence. For Topan, it is also one of the instruments which will kill independence:

Na kimojawapo cha vyombo hivyo ni Bunge lenye vyama vya siasa viwili kimoja cha serikali; cha pili kikiwa mkabala na serikali. Hivyo, mkoloni akikosa kunong'oneza huku, ananong'oneza kule. Kisu kweli hicho: kinamdhuru yeye mwenyewe Binadamu (Topan,1977:52).

Like the Assembly's two-party system: a pro-government party, an anti-government party... In the same way, the colonialist who doesn't succeed in whispering his advice here, can always go there... That's the knife: it wounds himself.

The colonialist mentality produces neo-colonialism (*ukolonimamboleo*) which affects all sectors of life, and manifests itself above all through economic individualism: everyone for himself - Kitaru's father's slogan. The whole text is interpreted through this grid. Kitaru imagines himself slicing through the heavens:

Ndiyo hivyo. Sasa sijui nililala saa ngapi. Lakini, mara ninaona nina manyoya. Mimi nimeota manyoya, mzee ameota manyoya; kila mtu na kila kitu kimeota manyoya: manyoya mengi sana. Mara manyoya yakageuka mbawa; tukawa tunaruka angani. Kwanza ilikuwa raha, raha kabisa. Lakini, mara tukaingiwa na hofu. Hatuwezi kufanya lolote. Mbawa zinaturusha zinapotaka. Vitu vinaruka angani. Majumba, magari, na sisi vinatupeperusha. Mimi, ninakumbuka, nilianza kuwa na hofu. Nikaanza kunyonyoa manyoya yangu,. Lakini kila nikijinyonyoa, mengine yanaota. Yananiziba pumzi. Mengine yanaota, makubwa zaidi na yenye nguvu zaidi kuliko yale ya mwanzo. Nikaanza kuingiwa na shaka. Shaka kweli. Mimi binadamu au ndege? Nikawa najiuliza na kufikiri. Wazee wangu wakamwita daktari. Naye daktari ana manyoya kama sisi; tena, yake ni mengi zaidi. Basi akaniambia ninadekeza akili yangu. Na nikaendelea kuwa na shaka kama nitakuwa na kiarusi... (MA:48-49)

I don't know at what time I fell asleep... I suddenly found I had feathers, my father had feathers, everyone, everything had feathers. Suddenly, these feathers became wings: we were flying in the air, first it was a pleasure, perfect pleasure. But, suddenly, there was fear. We couldn't do anything. The wings took us where they wanted. Things were flying: houses, cars; and we were also swept away. I remember that I started to be afraid. I started pulling out my feathers, but others grew in their place. They prevented me from breathing. Feathers were growing, bigger than the ones I had. I started doubting. Real doubts: was I a man or a bird? I asked myself. My parents called the doctor and he had feathers like me, more than me. He told me that I was self-satisfied. He told me that if I continued to doubt, I would become paralysed (kiarusi, a neck spasm caused by a pepo, a spirit, according to Sacleux, ar).

This beautiful lyrical passage is supposed to express "Kitaru's economic advancement" (Kiango, 1975:13), which remains a bit simplistic. Kitaru wants to change this society in which he does not feel comfortable: we know this, we know what he is thinking - seeing as the second part of the play takes place in his imagination. As for Juma, he likes chic hotels, and is not ready to fight for a new society. Nostalgia prevents him from progressing: he feels nostalgia rather than resentment, which also has a meaning which is as much poetic as political.

Kitabu hiki kina falsafa inayofaa sana, hasa kwa nchi kama Tanzania kwani mwandishi ameandika juu ya jambo linlomhusu kila Mtanzania. Kwa sababu ya umuhimu wa mchezo huu kwa kila Mtanzania, ndiyo hapa namlaumu mwandishi kwa kuandika Mashetani kama alivyoandika. Kwa sababu, ni watu wachache tu watakaouelewa kwa urahisi. Kwa wengi, unakuwa ni kama kujaribu kuvunja chuma kwa meno (Kiango, 1975:19)

This book contains a philosophy which is very useful in a country like Tanzania because the writer has written on things concerning every Tanzanian. Because of the importance of this play for every Tanzanian, I am critical of the writer for writing Mashetani the way he has done. Few people can understand it easily. For many, it will be like trying to break steel with one's teeth.

A strange compliment: the idea that the work is important for the very reason that it has been written this way does not occur to the critic. Political content is the essence: form would merely be the wrapping, which here is particularly complex. This division between form and content is fundamental to a certain literary instruction. Here it deals with a very contemporary work, of which the object is a reflection on the society in which author and critic live and work.

To subject the work to school scrutiny, to blame its author for not taking the pupils' level into account, is to deny him every quality as a writer: to present him as an author of examination questions and anthology excerpts, and not as a true poet, or a true dramatist. And yet, the fundamental position of Tanzanian or Kenyan criticism in Kiswahili is precisely what I have just described: the author is summoned before the commission of examinations, and is reprimanded for writing texts that are too complicated.

Jogoo Kijijini, Ngao ya Jadi

The thesis years in Berlin came to an end in 1973. Two years later, on 16 November 1975, in Dar es Salaam, Ebrahim Hussein himself interpreted two entirely original works, which showed a break with the epic dramatic art of the previous plays (Fiebach, 1993). He created a poetic theatre, a dramatic monologue borrowing from story-telling soirées, while constituting a radical innovation. Moreover, he wrote in free verse, showing research on rhythm departing from naturalist dialogues, even if *Mashetani* already allowed a few lyrical spurts.

Tanzanian criticism did not know about these plays; we had to wait more than ten years to read criticsm of them. This poetic theatre constitutes Hussein's latest style, and corresponds to a new vision of Tanzanian society. It is noteworthy that these texts are dedicated to the *wanakijiji* (villagers) of Mbambara, which was one of the first, and one of the most widely studied model villages of Tanzanian socialism. An article, *Mbambara, the long road to Ujamaa* (Cliffe et al,1975:370-390) chronicles this condensed version of Tanzanian history, which is present in Hussein's mind, since the argument of his next play, *Arusi*, will be drawn from an incident from the same village. It can be summarised as follows:

Mbambara is in the Bondei region, next to the Amboni plantations, 40 kms west of Tanga on the Mnyusi. It was the young TANU people at Muheza who decided to undertake this project in 1963. Twenty to sixty pioneers settled on the 4000 acres that had been entrusted to them. The first years were difficult but in 1967 the first sisal was harvested. However, the difficulties persisted, linked as they were to the absence of a collective spirit among the villagers, to the incompetence of those in charge, and to the inconsistency of a government incapable, for example, of settling the question of residential permits for non-Tanzanians. The party left the village to itself, whereas in the beginning relations were rather close, since the village leadership came from the TANU, links weakened and no political education took place any more. Of the initial 4000 acres, 3700 had not been cleared by 1972.

One then understands that Ebrahim the poet, the former militant student has a lot to say about this phase in his youth. It is understandable that he doesn't want to turn his topic into a cry of revolt which could become the watchword of a protest he sees coming but does not believe in. He does not see himself as a standard-bearer. He already has the feeling that his approach is misunderstood, even among the intellectual community with whom he has since shared the university adventure for more than a decade.

The reading of *Kinjeketile* contained the seeds of misunderstandings: a nationalistic epic led by a tragic hero. This hero is original in historical theatre dramas dominating African stages of the sixties, but he remained truly misunderstood. As for the demons, the *Mashetani*, they are numerous and widespread. The main body of the play contrasts traditional Africa with an Africa corrupted by neocolonialism, by the poison of foreign culture, distilled by education which makes the hero lose his head.

This interpretation puts aside the oeuvre's own movement and proposes a simplistic vision of the relationships between the two main characters. This type of reading, allegorical and de-contextualised at the same time, closely attached to the text, detaches the play from the author's other texts and refuses to ask the central question - that of the movement of the oeuvre, of its own development from one play to the next, in the Tanzanian and African context of the early seventies.

In this way, a curiously delaying effect is created: the oeuvre continues to be written in growing isolation, the plays are published, but are not performed, except by the author himself in 1975. Reviews are rare, to my knowledge, only Mutegi's work deals with *Arusi* in Kiswahili. The allegorical reading looks for the social or moral key and for a Tanzanian or Kenyan Marxist, it's often the same for all the characters. The new plays are not prescribed and the majority of pupils and students remain unaware of them.

Arusi

Arusi may be read in the light of the preceding path. The play is an effort to rediscover the political preoccupations of young people in a way which does not bear false political dynamics, or an old content; and which, at the same time, by-passes the impasse of the dramatic monologue by allowing group participation. He, therefore, invents a type of theatre which mixes portrayal (or even social satire) and the evocation of the dreams and disillusions of a generation. He tries to place himself on these two levels by combining realistic dialogue from Swahili life on the streets with the free verse from the attempts at poetic drama.

Jogoo Kijijini and Ngao ya Jadi

We are in the Swahili environment of a Mombasa neighbourhood, the same as that of the first plays. The parents of the bride are in need of money, and must borrow in order to provide a beautiful ceremony. The groom has gone to foreign lands to seek his fortune: his absence leads to catastrophe and his wife is made pregnant by another man. The happy life dreamt of at the beginning is not to be; what emerges, are a few lyrical outbursts of feeling from the young friends of the married couple.

Hussein portrays idealistic young people, lovesick dreamers like Ali who seduces the abandoned spouse, or Kahinja who leaves for Tanzania to build socialism, and returns, as we shall see in the last chapter. Young, at loose ends, and dreamers, they live in the streets, in groups, sharing the same secrets, the same irresponsibility, similar to those young Lebanese whose life stories are told by Michael Gilsenan in *Recognising Islam* (1982:120-124).

The author also shows us household life, particularly the relationships between a young woman and her initiation godmother, and those between guests invited to a marriage. As always, Hussein knows how to make his female characters speak, and his dialogues ring true. *Arusi* borrows from the preceding dramaturgical modes: the picture of the Mombasa Swahili background reminds one of *Wakati Ukuta,* the poetic effusions of the young idealists have been written like *Jogoo Kijijini.*

The dramatist has made an effort to produce a synthesis between the different modes of dramatic expression he has practised. The result is a work which is concise and ambitious, elliptical and filled with references to the contemporary world. At the same time it is a difficult work which only aggravated the intellectual gulf between Hussein and the critics.

Academic criticism obviously plays a central role in Swahili literature since, in a way, it gives the work a stamp of acceptability for schools - which ensures its commercial success. Moreover, the play has been structured in a rather complex way, and may disconcert the reader and put off a potential theatre director. Indeed, all the action takes place in the imagination of Mwanaheri, the heroine who dreams about her married life, since she cannot make it a reality.

> *Hiki ni kivuli cha shaka. Mwanaheri anaingiwa na shaka katika kitambo kifupi anapofumba macho. Hafurahi kama tunavyotarajia baada ya kuvishwa pete na kuahidiwa ndoa. Kivuli hiki cha shaka kinamfanya atafakari maisha yake ya ndoa na Bukini ambaye anaondoka na anayeona kitu chenyewe kuwa kama mchezo tu ijapokuwa ameikubali hiyo ahadi* (Mutegi, 19855:146).

There is the shadow of doubt. Mwanaheri is overcome by doubts during a brief moment while closing her eyes. She is not overjoyed, as we expect, after slipping on the ring and contracting the marriage. This shadow of doubt makes her think about her married life with Bukini, who leaves and doesn't take it seriously, even if he accepts the contract.

Katika onyesho la pili, anaona vile sherehe za ndoa zingekuwa. Onyesho la nne tunapewa maadalizi ya Bibi Arusi na mafunzo anayopewa (Mutegi, 1985:147).

In the second scene she sees how the marriage celebration would unfold. In the fourth scene, we are shown the bride's preparations and we hear the instructions she is given.

For the critic, this dramatic complexity would be at the service of a social message about the necessity of living according to one's means:

Ndoa sharti izingatie uhalisi wa maisha ya kijamii. Kwa hivyo Hussein anapinga sherehe za ndoa ambazo haziambatani na uwezo wa kiuchumi wa wanaohusika. Anapinga sherehe ghali-ghali zenye kuingiza watu katika madeni (Mutegi, 1985:148).

Marriage should take into account the reality of social life; therefore, Hussein criticises marriages that are not in keeping with the financial means of those concerned. He criticises luxurious celebrations which put families into debt.

This message is full of good sense - but why use so much dramatic subtlety for such moralising platitude? - would, in fact cover a political idea having to do with relations between Kenya and Tanzania... That would thus be the reason for the complex fable, we are told. It's worth quoting the page which Mutegi devotes to this rather surprising but very revealing analysis about this hermeneutic mode of understanding texts:

Husseini anajadili matatizo yanayozikabili nchi mbili, Kenya na Tanzania katika kushirikiana kiuchumi, kisiasa na kijamii. Matatizo haya yana asili yake katika mifumo ya kiuchumi na kiitikadi inayotofautiana katika nchi hizi. Kenya inataka Tanzania ifungue mpaka wake lakini Tanzania haitaki kwa sababu ya kufahamu matatizo ambayo yanaweza kutokea. Uhusiano huu unaelezwa kwa jazanda ya pendekezo la arusi ambalo halizingatii uhalisi unaohusu jamii zinazohusika. Hivyo Tanzania haina budi kuahirisha (sic?) mapatano haya hadi hali itakapobadilika. Mwandishi anatueleza hali hii kwa kutuonyesha, katika jazanda ya arusi, kwamba ndoa ni jambo muhimu ambalo halipaswi kurukiwa kwa pupa (Mutegi, 1985:149).

Hussein discusses the difficulties of political, economic and social cooperation between the two countries. These problems have their origin in the economic and ideological structures differentiating these countries. Kenya wants Tanzania to open its border; but Tanzania refuses because it realises the problems that may follow. This relationship can be explained by the metaphor of marriage which does not consider the reality of co-existing communities. Tanzania doesn't need to change the treaties before the situation can be transformed. The writer explains this situation by showing us, thanks to the metaphor of marriage, that the latter is an important thing that should not be taken lightly.

The above is the conclusion of Mutegi's analysis, written in Kiswahili and found in the Nairobi University library. The volume is in a pitiful state, dirtied and annotated by a multitude of hands; it is clear that numerous students have consulted it. What's more, I was told about this analysis by people I spoke to on a daily basis.

The author did not hesitate before the necessity to interpret; but he has recourse to the theory of keys instead of trying to place the work within the continuity of a literary project. "*Hatuna budi kumlaumu Hussein*" – "*we must blame Hussein*" (Mutegi:ibid). The complex structure of the work, the effort to give a visual status to the flux of conscience, to dreams, the poetic prose, the lyrical effusions: all support this project. Hussein was criticised by Kiango for the complexity of *Mashetani* and he is reprimanded by Mutegi for the complexity of *Arusi*; the silence which greeted *Jogoo Kijijini* and *Ngao ya Jadi* and *Kwenye Ukingo wa Thim* is the worst criticism.

In his last play, he partially breaks with free verse, and rediscovers the natural dialogue of the first plays while forcing himself to take into account the supernatural dimensions of the narratives, integrating them with popular mythological conceptions. The play's argument is taken from an incident, bringing two conceptions of tradition into play. I found no review of them, although at least two books have been published on the Otieno case, the name under which this incident is known (Médard,1987).

This deafening silence surrounds a work which is perfectly in line with Hussein's general themes, and which looks at questions of identity in a pessimistic and penetrating way, as I will try to show in the next chapter. In 1996 an excellent translation (Njogu, 1996) of the play was circulating: is it a sign indicating a new interest in Ebrahim Hussein's work?

5
Being Swahili

Ebrahim Hussein's plays resound with theoretical debates on the building of socialism, although they carefully avoid tackling them head on. These texts are situated in a political context, which must be borne in mind when reading them. They were produced within the framework of a university theatre during a period of intense debates on the "Hill", as Tanzanians called the University of Dar es Salaam.

In the years following the Arusha Declaration (1967) the two plays which made Hussein known to the public were produced, expressing what I would call his political voluntarism. In *Arusi* in 1980, he submerges himself in the universe of coastal Swahili and Arab culture, signalling a return to the very roots of identity at the same time as he was undergoing a radical questioning of power. The last play, which was published in 1988, *Kwenye Ukingo wa Thim,* places the ethnic question front-stage.

We witness a metaphysical deepening of Ebrahim Hussein's thinking, and a return (although with a slight shift) to the question of identity. This matter is presented in an explicit way through several characters. Kitaru in *Mashetani* and Chris in *Kwenye Ukingo wa Thim* both ask themselves who they are. Other characters dream about their lives in *Arusi*, or are possessed like *Kinjeketile*. These frequent dual personalities, dreamed existences and crises of possession are symptomatic of a questioning, the meaning of which is to be found in Hussein's aesthetic and literary undertaking, and also in his own situation during the first twenty-five years of Tanzanian independence. The shifting of the notion of Swahili identity, which was produced in the course of these years, had a profound effect on his oeuvre, and helps to explain its orientation, although it can also give rise to a certain lack of understanding. The first play exploits the framework of Dar's Swahili milieu, which Hussein knows and in which the young writer lived towards the end of the sixties. The characters are firmly drawn; there is no ambiguity as regards their acts or their relationships. This clarity, this false clarity, which is partially a rhetorical effect produced by Hussein's chosen genre, will never be seen again, but it is a good idea to pause on it.

"Place: the action takes place in a provincial capital along the coast, Dar, Tanga, Bagamoyo. Time: the present" (WU:8)

The characters paint a social background. The dramatic conflict has been interpreted in terms of cultural conflict (Mcha, 1977) between different communities, while for Hussein, the individual dimension is essential. However, they are youthful works in which the dominant trait is the author's dramatic virtuosity.

Kinjeketile is an ambitious play. We know that this revolt is a part of Tanzania's nationalistic, heroic exploits, after having given rise to epics in Kiswahili. Hussein proposes to depict for us the circumstances of the *Wamatumbi* under colonial domination between 1890 and 1904, and their defence actions. At the beginning of the play, we are among the *Warufiji*, who share the labour and the misfortune of the members of the neighbouring tribes: *Wabichi*, *Wazaramo*, all at work on the plantations. These groups confer together on how to put an end to their exploitation. Kinjeketile does not appear, but we learn that he is in his hut, conferring with the spirit of the waters.

At the beginning of Act 2, Kinjeketile comes out of his hut, possessed by the spirit; he advances slowly, not seeing anyone, as he wanders over the grounds. The sunlight strikes him and he launches into a long, inspired speech in which he catches a glimpse of the luminous tomorrows which the water will bring. He predicts the departure of the Germans and the arrival of Seyyid Said, the Sultan of Zanzibar, who has just accepted the English protectorate and has ceded the coast to the Germans (Polenyk, 1985). When he recovers his spirits once again, he is shattered to learn what he has predicted; but the harm has been done. They prepare for war, sustained by a belief in the invulnerability procured by water. When consulted by the chiefs of the neighbouring tribes, Kinjeketile assures them that the spirit of the water which possesses him is the same as that which they venerate under a different name. Yet, mobilization frightens him: he predicts that the "word created by a man may make a slave out of he who begot it". Many words were created after Arusha.

The revolt started despite Kinjeketile's ritual taboos. The house of an Arab is the first to be pillaged. The Germans take up position in their small forts, their *bomas*: the fighters launch an attack and are massacred by the force of the European fire, against which the sacred water is not of great help. The war is recounted to us by a narrator: he never appears. A prisoner of the Germans is summoned by guards to reveal that the magical nature of the water was a hoax, but he refuses. His consent would have permitted the captives to be released. He accepts to die, leaving the myth intact; sacrificing this generation of fighters in the name of future liberation.

Kinjeketile, inspired, is beside himself. The charismatic leader is possessed. The man who dreams about a Tanganyika becoming Swahililand in the future only dreams the dream when in a trance. His dream is first of all that of an end to tribalism, - the central theme of his vaticinations. The differences and conflicts are a reality in the play and the author indicates the different Swahili accents between the ethnic groups. In an introductory note, omitted in the English edition, the author points out that the *Wamatumbi* pronounce the 'r' like an 'l' and thus say *nzuli* instead of *nzuri*. Several retorts mark the less than affable feelings that some ethnic groups harbour against others.

Lakini toka lini Mmatumbi akawa shujaa? (KI:5)
Since when was a Mmatumbi a hero?

A *Mzaramo* remarks treacherously, which elicits this reply:
Hatukuja hapa kugombana juu ya kabila (KI:6).
We are not here to quarrel about our tribes.

This play represents a considerable deepening of Hussein's conceptions of drama. It's an ambitious and complex work. One could say that the misunderstanding with the critics starts with this first work and only gets worse.

Binadamu huzaa neno ... likamuangusha aliyelizaa (KI:36)
Man creates a word ... which brings about the downfall of him who created it.

Initially, these groups are identified: *Mkichi, Mzaramo, Mmatumbi, Mrufiji*. The sun must lighten up the eyes of every member of these groups and, later, they will form only one:

Tutakuwa watu wa Seyyd Said (KI:15)
We will be the people of Seyyd Said

Sijali kuchukiwa na wewe (kwa pole pole kama anasema na mtoto). Haina maana kupata uhulu ili baadaye tuwe watumwa wa mabwana wengine, watupande vichwani na kututumia wapendavyo. Ikiwa huyu Seyyid Said anaweza kutumiliki akili zetu bila sisi wenyewe kujua, akaweza kututumia bila kujua, basi yeye ni adui mkubwa kuliko Njelumani (KI:27)

It's not important to me if you do hate me (he speaks meekly as if he is talking to a child). If this Seyyid Said could, without our realising it, enslave us, body and mind, he would be a far worse enemy than the Germans. He could rule us without setting foot in this country.

Ikiwa ni Hongo, kwa nini anasema baadaye tutakuwa watu wa Seyyid Said? Kwa nini anataka kutuuza sisi watoto wake kwa mabwana wengine. Na nikiacha anipande ninakuwa siwezi kujua. (KI:27)

If it was Hongo, why did he say that we shall be children of Seyyid Said? Why is he selling us, his own people, to another master... These are difficult questions... When I let him possess me, he robs me of my thinking power.

Sisi tunamuamini Kolelo. Tunaweza kumfuata Kolelo tu. Lakini kila tukisikia zaidi habari za huyu Hongo tunaona kuwa huyu Hongo kwa kweli ni Kolelo. Kolelo anakaa majini, na huyu vile vile... Lakini nywiywila imesema kuwa yeye ni Hongo. Tumekuja kuwauliza: Huyu ni Kolelo, au ni Hongo? Au majina yote ni ya mtu mmnoja? Kolelo na Hongo kwa kweli ni wamoja, kama wanavyosema watu wengine huko kwetu, basi sisi tuko tayari kuwa pamoja na nyinyi... (KI:31)

We believe in Kolelo. We can only follow his guidance. But the more we hear of your spirit Hongo the more we are convinced that he is Kolelo. Kolelo lives in the water. And so does this one too.

But the nywiywila (rumour) has it that he is Hongo. We come to ask you whether this is Kolelo or Hongo, whether these two names belong to the same spirit? If it is so, then we are ready to join you. If not, then we cannot fight together.

This return of the Sultan is a strange prophecy, made in standard Swahili by the charismatic leader of the Bantu rebellion. What meaning should be given to this prediction? It marks the presence of the Arabs, the paradoxal unifiers of the continent thanks to Kiswahili, and at the same time the first victims of the revolt. Thus, from the start, Zanzibar and the Arabs appear as imaginary actors in the foreground of Ebrahim Hussein's oeuvre. From the start a tragic message is delivered. Political power is a type of madness: it alienates identity and, yet, this alienation enables one to surpass oneself. Politics is the domain of the imagination and of dreams, and power confines one to madness.

Shakespeare, translated into Kiswahili by Julius Nyerere, already had a glimpse of these dimensions of our existence. Seyyid Said's implication in the play signals the eruption of Arabs from Zanzibar in Hussein's dramas. Their return would be the sign of a new oppression for Kinjeketile the 'messiah'. In fact, at the beginning of the century, they renounced their sovereignty on the coast, following a series of one-sided treaties with the Germans. Can a native from Kilwa whose patronymic name evokes the prophet, and whose grandfather was a respected leader of a brotherhood easily settle his account with history, and distance himself that much from the former suzerainty, Zanzibar? This question is at the heart of Swahili identity.

Waarabu walipokuja walileta ustaarabu wa kiarabu na biashara ya kishenzi ya utumwa. Kwa watu wengine, dini ya kiislamu isingeenea huku kwetu ila kuja kwa Waarabu. Hussein katika kuwachora watawala hawa wawili haoni yupi aliye mzuri zaidi. Ndipo Kinjeketile anaposita (Sengo, 1975:18).

When the Arabs came, they brought their culture and the savage slave trade. For some, Islam would not have spread in our country if the Arabs hadn't come. In describing these two types of domination, Hussein doesn't know which is the better; that is where Kinjeketile hesitates.

Islam came with culture and slavery... And this set-up produced the Swahili culture. Thus, Arab domination had ambiguous effects. One of the most brilliant is surely the development of this language which is Kiswahili, which has become a literary language, producing literary theory, and, on top of that, in the footsteps of Ebrahim Hussein's works...

Seyyid Said hakutajwa kama mwarabu tu bali kama shetani alivyo shetani mkoloni mwingine yeyote. Kutajwa kwake kulichokoza hisi za watu...Tungeweza tukamlaumu Hussein kwa kumtaja Seyyid Said kuwa mtu maarufu katika historia ya Afrika Mashariki, na asituambie vile alivyoathiri na kudhalilisha maisha ya Waafrika wa pwani ya mashariki ya bara la Afrika. Kwa kuyafanya haya, Mwandishi ameweza kulichora jambo kubwa lionekane dogo, kwa bahati mbaya, hatukubali kuliona dogo kwa vile linavyotuumiza vichwa kwa kujiuliza maswali na kukereza akili zetu kwa kulifikiria. (Sengo, 1975:18).

Seyyid Said is not mentioned as an Arab but, indeed, as any other colonising demon. It hurts people's feelings to have him mentioned... We could blame Hussein for mentioning Seyyid Said, as an important man in East Africa's history, and for not telling us how he affected and oppressed the lives of Africans of the Eastern coast of the African continent. By doing so, the writer underplayed an important episode, and unfortunately we don't accept taking it lightly, because of how it gives us headaches thinking about it.

One must quote Seyyid Said and condemn the feudal potentate. Hussein is accused of being too discreet, too fatalistic, he accepts going from the Germans to the Arabs, jumping out of the frying pan and into the fire. I think that the discretion he is accused of comes from the fact that he also sees the Arab presence as being a constituent element of his identity, and of the world he claims to come from. It serves no purpose to rail against one's ancestors. As Cesaire has taught us, they may become twice as ferocious. Nevertheless, like Cesaire, our author clearly insists on saying that he is opposed to their feudal and pro-slavery power.

These reflections are continued in the following play, *Mashetani*, the action of which is situated in time between the 1964 Zanzibar revolution and the Arusha Declaration of 1967. It deals with the conflicts between social classes in the new Tanzania. The feudal landowners have been chased from Zanzibar, Said's heirs have not taken power. Is this new bureaucratic bourgeoisie (one of its sons is the main character of the play) the reincarnation of the feudal landowners? The problem is posed via a discussion between two students: Juma, who comes from Zanzibar where his family owns plantations, and Kitaru, a child of the new bureaucratic strata. The dramatisation of the conflict implies identity loss and transformation.

Juma embodies the slightly cynical scepticism of the aristocrats who've lost their place, while Kitaru is not yet as avid as the new social classes who are about to monopolise the state, but already shows some signs, despite his malady, of having the disposition to acquire it. The questions on social and personal identity intersect intimately. In *Kinjeketile*, the group representatives were busy forging a new identity for themselves in combat; here, two young intellectuals confront Zanzibar's revolution and the setting up of a system which is socialist and bureaucratic at the same time, creating perceptible distance from the start, between discourse and practice.

The demon speaks his own language, but, while Hongo makes Kinjeketile speak Kiswahili the demon's language is incomprehensible gibberish. The future is dark. As the doctor who has been called to Kitaru's bedside says:

Wasi wasi una hatari zaidi kuliko ugonjwa (MA:34)
Doubt is more pernicious than illness.

The play presents debates on the nature of the new Tanzanian society and on the formation of social classes in a socialist society. Juma has been raised in an atmosphere of longing for the good old days, but a new world is dawning before the students. As Hussein says in his introduction, the students embody the quest of the individual in the world, but in a world full of problems, particularly that of tribalism.

The students were full of illusions, they thought that "all they had to do, was to fight against tribalism and religious prejudices" (KI, VI).

Today, the political plan is to clip the wings of all the Kitarus who are preparing to take flight. The demon is the game-leader: Juma has come to resemble him. To make Kitaru's truth materialise, Juma must lose his identity, to reveal the new class to itself, he must lose himself. The demon's purpose is to reveal Kitaru's limitations - Kitaru has become *Binadamu,* Man.

The demon questions Kitaru before he dies. He asks Kitaru to celebrate his death; Kitaru chooses a waltz, which is far removed from the Swahili *beni ngoma.* Kitaru wonders about the future:

Sasa lililobaki ni azimio... Kwa hivyo, nina haja ya vitu vitatu: bidii, ari, na ukweli. Ukweli ndiyo upi? Mimi ni nani? (MA:11)

We need a resolution now... I thirst for three things: diligence, determination, truth. What is truth? Who am I?

The choice of terms, particularly that of *Azimio,* evoking the Arusha Declaration, the birth of Tanzanian socialism, is obviously not left to chance. It must be remembered that it is the average man, *Binadamu,* who, confronted by the demon, asks himself certain questions - and to which the only solution is a declaration - the effects of which will be felt in action.

Kuna kitendo na mtendaji: vitu hivi ni kitu kimoja (MA:12)
There is action, and the doer: these are interrelated.

The play is an illustration of this proposal. The discussions between the two students help us understand the meaning of Juma's demonic nature. He has no illusions about the university; he needs a degree to earn money. As for Kitaru, he's looking for truth: he is an idealist confronted by Juma the demon's slightly cynical speech.

Ukweli, bwana, degree inakupa tonge ya wali na mchuzi, tena mchuzi wa kuku, badala ya tonge ya ugali na maharagwe... (MA:17)

The truth, my man, is a degree that will enable you to afford a meal of rice and chicken soup, instead of mere maize meal with beans.

The students question the meaning of their studies and their action. If university makes bourgeois of them, why does the socialist state build a university? To search for truth, Kitaru would say, but that makes Juma (or rather the demon he represents) laugh.

Toka tumepata uhuru, sisi Waafrika hapa imekuwa kama tumeingia ehe, mfano mzuri, imekuwa kama tumeingia katika jahazi moja zuri sana na jina letu limeandikwa... Nahodha nani? (MA:21)

Since we've become independent, it is as if we Africans were - it is a good example - in a fine boat, with our name on it... But who is in charge?

The current sweeps the boat away in one direction, while the captain wants it to go in another. The current sweeps the boat away to the isle of demons - the father, humming *I like Some Money* in English enters at that moment - and nobody knows where the captain wants to go. As for the passengers, do they know where they want to go? Juma wants to be lucid, while Kitaru continues the discussion without succeeding in reconciling his actions and his ideas. He expresses almost admiring surprise, or even a certain fascination in Juma's presence. As his father says:

Si ajabu babu yake alikuwa na watumwa (MA:26)
Isn't it incredible to think that his grandfather had slaves...

Kitaru cannot come to terms with the growing contradiction between what he thinks - the search for truth and for the meaning of life - and that which he experiences every day: money, and now a Mercedes Benz. He escapes into illness, into a sort of neurosis of doubt. His identity wavers when confronted with the conflicts provoked by his group's accession to power.

Ana ugonjwa wa wasi wasi... (MA:39)
He suffers from the disease of doubt...

Juma is stronger; he gives the impression of having understood what happened before, and what is happening now. Are the ramblings of his grandmother, who knows so well how to tell stories (*hadithi*) about the good old days, poison or proof of love? "Mara nyingi, mapenzi hugeuka sumu", "love is often transformed into poison" (MA:42). What can he explain to Kitaru, if the latter cannot understand on his own (MA:44)? And yet, Juma's grandmother represents wisdom: she knows that the demon can take all shapes (MA:28). But then, Kitaru is truly ill, as shown by the consultation with the doctor sent for by his parents.

Anataka wewe umwambie yeye anaumwa na nini (MA:34)
He wants you to tell him what he is suffering from.

Labda, kwake yeye, ninavyofikiri mimi wasiwasi una hatari zaidi kuliko ugonjwa (MA:34)

Perhaps, in his case, I think doubt is more dangerous than disease.

The grandmother represents another form of illusion: that of 'paternalism', linked to a materialism which is at least as strong as that of the Mercedes Benz owner, Kitaru's father humming about his love for money.

Yeye akiwa na mapenzi na wewe Mungu atakupa zaidi ya hayo (MA:38)
He may have his Mercedes; but God will give you more than that.

In a bar, Juma listens to drunks expounding the new-world law: the African must drink beer, eat well, sleep well, live in a nice house and be surrounded by pretty women. That is the radiant future Juma wants to expound, the vanity of which he understands perfectly, and which Kitaru cannot understand. Juma is the mediator between real life, that of their parents and their car, the drunkards with their beer, the grandmother with her slaves, and intellectual life, that of history and law at the university. For him, knowledge is acquired through games or dreams:

Katika maisha ya ndoto, mtu anaona ukweli zaidi kuliko katika maisha ya ukweli (MA:47)
In dreams, man gets to know reality better than in real life.

Kitaru is the illustration of this proposal: faced with the contradiction between his dreams and his situation, he dreams that he becomes a bird. He is no longer possessed as Kinjeketile was by the water spirit; he escapes from this world like a bird, he becomes covered in feathers, and the feathers become wings.

> *Nikaanza kuingiwa na shaka: mimi ni binadamu au ndege?* (MA:49)
> I began to have doubts: am I a human being, or a bird?

> *Ujuzi unakusanya haya yote, unachuja haya yote, na kuambatanisha na kitendo* (MA:52)
> Cognizance garners all this; analyses it, and links it all with action.

> *Kitaru: Yote yalianza katika mchezo.*
> *Juma: Yote yalianza katika hadithi.*
> *Kitaru : Ukitaka hivyo basi, yote yalianza katika kitendo* (MA:56)
> Kitaru: It all started as a game.
> Juma: It all started with a story.
> Kitaru: If that is the case, then it all started with action.

> *Hatuwezi kuacha hadithi za jana zitawale roho zetu* (MA:57)
> We cannot allow stories of yesteryear to take control of our souls.

Truth can only be told in a game; Kitaru and Juma must take parts in order to say what is essential. The demon could be called the principle of reality, cupidity, materialism. One needs to play-act in order to make him appear as a dominating force. All in all, under the socialist power which is being set up, and despite declarations, the demon of cupidity is watching.

Hussein proposes a metaphysical vision of social reality, and of the conflicts that span it. Amongst these conflicts is one which is not mentioned as such, but which is present in the background: Juma must belong to the group of *Waswahili* Arabs, while Kitaru belongs to the new social class which has taken possession of the state, and which we may also define as Swahili. What the *Waswahili* Arabs know, their *ujuzi*, that knowledge born of the experience of life and history, the new *Waswahili* do not understand. The play concludes with a break between the two friends.

Tanzanian identity is carried by the new class taking power, and to which neither Hussein nor his characters belong. He is not a member of the group of planters exiled from Zanzibar, either.

He returns to social reality with *Arusi*, which was published in 1980. The type of writing in this play is rather different from that of the previous plays: the author is not generous with stage directions or an introduction. What's more, the language is often poetical and metaphorical, and the text is printed in the form of free verse. This play did not give rise to many reviews; I have offered an interpretation of this situation (Ricard, 1991).

We are not in the interior, nor in the capital of the country, but on the coast, in the birthplace of Swahili culture, in an unidentified place, probably a village on the Kenyan coast. For the first time, Hussein situates the action in a milieu, which could be his own: that of coastal Swahili culture - authentic Swahili culture - as Harries would say. The reflection on tribalism, which was presented as the central argument of the preceding texts, seems to have been eliminated from this work. Instead of the conflicts being presented and overtaken by prophecy or games, here they are supposed to be prevented because we are in a homogeneous cultural milieu of which the marriage rites are those of the *Waswahili*. In short, the choice of scene already constitutes a stance on this side of state and national reality. The scene is not even situated in a particular country. On the other hand, the culture referred to is very much that of the Swahili: coastal, urban, convivial.

Arusi

At the start of the play, in front of the curtain, Mwanaheri and Bukini get engaged, then Bukini leaves. The rest of the play, which begins with their marriage, is the dream of their life: it thus takes place in their imagination. In the second scene, the party is in full swing. In the third scene, the husband's brother prepares his departure: he also wants to get away from the village and to go elsewhere.

Wanasema kuna fikira mpya huko...

They say there are some new ideas over there...

The marriage ceremonies continue with the participation of the villagers, including Bwana Mzuri, who embodies the big land owners. In the second act, we meet the village youngsters who do not really take part in the ceremonies. They envy those who are leaving. Kahinja, who dreams of leaving, sings about his dreams to the audience. In the third act Mwanaheri, the wife, who stayed behind in the village after Bukini's departure for the Emirates, the new promised land, secretly talks with Ali who, one guesses, is her lover. She is pregnant: the neighbours and the family are moved by the situation. In the fourth act, Kahinja has come back to see his family, Mwanaheri and his friends. Mwanaheri awaits her husband's return, and learns that Kahinja has been arrested for having dipped into the cash box of the *ujamaa* village he left for (he thus went to mainland Tanzania). At the end of the play, Ali, Mwanaheri's lover, leaves to join Bukini. The last scene shows us the two fiances who have stopped acting. Mwanaheri slips off her engagement ring; she is frightened of the demon of love.

We are back in reality. We are really in the heart of Swahili culture, but that culture is no longer a living reality for the young people drinking whisky and leaving for the Emirates or Tanganyika (sic). The youngsters have no future on the coast. What do they have left, while the old folks try their best to perpetuate rites which slowly lose their meaning? Bukini has left for the Arab countries in the Gulf to look for a good job; Kahinja, the idealist, has gone to the neighbouring socialist country, attracted by the 'cool breeze' of new ideas, as he says himself; but he gets nothing from it. On the contrary, he finds himself in prison and certainly does not set an example to follow.

In this Swahili world, the forces of dissolution are no longer called tribalism: they're economic, they oblige young people to become expatriates. *Arusi*'s world only appears to be that of an identity fallback; the old identity, that of the coast, is no more than a folkloric dream in which young people can no longer participate.

This questioning of identity among intellectuals can again be found in Hussein's latest play, *Kwenye Ukingo wa Thim* (1988). While the tribalism is considered by the author to be one of the essential themes of his first works it seems to have been forgotten in *Arusi*, it becomes the central problem of this play. The central characters, Herbert and

Martha, have followed the advice given by Ngugi, and quoted by Hussein. Herbert, the Luo, has married the Gikuyu, Martha. The differences between Swahili Luo and Gikuyu should no longer matter; they should disappear in the same way the differences between the Warufiji, the Wamatumbi and the Wagogo disappeared. Yet, it is not the case.

We are in Kenya, a country where Kiswahili did not play the same role in the construction of unity as in Tanzania. Here, Hussein deals in Kiswahili with a milieu speaking English in everyday life. Today, Kiswahili has reached its maturity: it can give an account of a world which is no longer that of the language's origin, the history of Tanzania, the sixties, the student environment, the coastal cities. Nairobi is a great, modern capitalist metropolis. The economic failure of socialism corresponds with the cultural failure of capitalism, since the cultural elite is not able to impose its point of view, and becomes the victim of the most retrograde customs, when it is not their carrier.

The play's argument was taken from a news item, which was the talk of of the town in Kenya. Mrs Otieno, the wife of a famous barrister of Luo origin had to leave her husband's body with the clan he came from; she was of Gikuyu origin, and their marriage represented a rare (but ill-accepted) case of interbreeding, since she could not assert her rights as a spouse in a Christian marriage and choose the place of her husband's burial. She appeals to magistrates, who agree with custom, and against her.

Kwenye Ukingo wa Thim (At the Edge of Thim)

The play begins in the house of Herbert, a barrister, at a time when everybody is preparing to welcome the son, who is back from the United States where he is furthering his studies. The family has gathered and the brother of the lady of the house, a Gikuyu, praises tribalism. This elicits jokes from Herbert, who disappears at the end of the scene, not to be seen again.

In the second act, we are in Herbert's village, in Luo country, near Lake Victoria. The old folks think that Herbert's body belongs to them, and Martha opposes this. In act three, we're back in Herbert's house. The brother-in-law wants to impose clan law on Martha; the members of the clan, who are furious about this resistance, come to destroy and pilfer from their 'brother's house'. Everything belongs to them, and the wife has no right to anything! Finally, in the last act, everything seems to collapse: the girlfriend of Chris, the son of the house, leaves him and returns to the United States. Chris stays behind alone. Maybe he embodies a form of hope.

The author places this text under the *Chira* sign, a Luo concept he considers similar to the Greek concept of *Nemesis*, the goddess who punishes hubris, the excesses shown by man. Yet, of what excesses are these heroes guilty? What destiny did they want to pursue and which furies forced them? Is it for having tried to forget clan, blood and soil laws?

Martha is a freedom fighter, a former *Mau-Mau*; she did not fight for a *Mau-Mau* or Gikuyu republic, but for a country in which the laws would guarantee the rights of the citizen against the demands of soil and blood. Yet, it's this ideal world dreamed of by the political and intellectual elite, by the nationalists of the Independence which collapses before the violence of the crowd and the indifference of the representatives of law and of state. Once again, the problems of political identity come to the fore, but in a less metaphorical way than in the first plays.

In Herbert's house, jokes are made about tribalism in the relationships between Gikuyu and Luo, but Martha's brother, a Gikuyu, cannot tolerate the Mswahili Ali's demonstration of identity in the wearing of an authentic costume. The Gikuyu bourgeois declares without beating around the bush:

Hatuna identity, sisi (KU:13)
The rest of us have no identity!

Who is *sisi*? Who does *"the rest of us"* include? The Gikuyu? The bourgeois? The intellectuals? We must remember that we are not in Tanzania, and that the fact of speaking Kiswahili is not a voluntary demonstration of national identity, as in *Kinjeketile*. Twenty years after independence, there exists a new bourgeoisie in Kenya who cannot pretend to represent the whole nation.

Kiswahili is now an element of dramatic convention. The

demarcation of identities is reintroduced. The Luo speak Kiswahili with their accent, indicated by particularities of pronunciation transcribed in Kiswahili. Identity becomes the space where violence takes place, not a founding violence, as that we caught a glimpse of in *Kinjeketile*, but a violence destroying the inter-ethnic, convivial sociability established in the Herbert household.

Wewe uko na sisi au wewe uko na wao? (KU:23)
Are you with us or with them?

Such is the law of the clan, the law of all who dream of ethnic cleansing, and to which the question of the Independence dream child, Chris, comes as a response:

Ma, mimi ni nani? (KU:2)
Ma, who am I?

The world collapsed under the blows of identity - violence which the volunteers of the nationalist struggle thought they had eradicated. Hussein reveals this sad assessment to us in his latest work. He has left Chris in vain on sentry duty for future struggles; the balance sheet is truly tragic.

On the coast, the fusion between 'Swahiliness' and 'Arabness' was accomplished. But closing ranks around one's identity is but a dream when faced with the economic pressures forcing young people to emigrate. In the cities, tribalism is resurfacing with the intellectuals. As the American girl friend says in the end:

(Jean) Ugomvi baina ya makabila sielewi. Pasta anayeamini mazingaombwe! Maiti, ambayo ni muhimu kuliko mtu aliye hai! Watu wa pekee hawa! (KU:38)

I can't understand the tribal conflict! A superstitious pastor! A dead body that is more important than the living! These are strange people!

The question of Swahili identity is at the heart of our questions on Ebrahim Hussein's oeuvre, but it seldom comes up in reviews, except at the time of the first works (*Wakati Ukuta*). It is asked against the background of historical development. Moreover, this oeuvre is part of more than two decades of Tanzanian socialism. These two histories - that of identity and of power – have thus to be articulated in order to understand the development of the oeuvre, and the questions it asks the reader today.

In the eyes of the specialists, soon after Independence, Swahili language and literature formed the foundation of an identity which had its territory on the coast, but which had no political power. In 1964, Harries, a specialist of Swahili poetry, could write:

Hata ungeenda juu, kiboko, makazi yako ni pwani...
Even though you go up-country, hippopotamus, your real habitation is at the coast...

Even though Swahili language and culture are now facing the mainland, turned away as it were from the coast and from the sea route and from Arabia, the real home of Swahili language and culture is still on the coast (Harries, 1964:229).

Ethnic identity, however vague it was, was linguistic identity. Almost ten years later, Eastman, a linguist herself, feeling that the definition of Swahili had changed, proposed a hypothesis on 'Swahiliness' by distinguishing several cultural types. The Mswahili (plural: WaSwahili) is the one reuniting these criteria: he's Muslim, bears an Arabic patronymic name, was born on the coast. We then have the following grid: the non-Muslim Swahili call Arabs Swahili Muslims, the Swahili Muslims call the others Africans. The non-Muslims confuse the Arabs and the other Muslims (Eastman, 1971).

Soon after, Arens showed that the Swahili identity had become the sign of belonging to a reference group of detribalised Tanzanians, situated in the political space opened up by national construction.

The variability of cultural traits, not uniformity, might be considered to be the hallmark of this ethnic group (Arens, 1974:431). The word "Swahili" (is) associated with the developing political culture of the new Tanzanian state (Arens, ibid:434).

The equation, 'ethnic group equals language', is not valid, on the contrary it is the national language, Kiswahili, which becomes the support of a new identity, in a way a naturalised Tanzanian identity is linked to a power of state. A small group from the coast with a complex history, but linked, above all to Islam, gave birth to the Swahili language. From it developed a Swahili identity which was appropriated by social groups linked to the development of a new political conscience: detribalised, often Islamised, urbanised and linked to the new economic networks which were being put into place. The fascinating studies carried out at Ujiji, bridgehead of the Zanzibari slave-traders on Lake Tanganyika, clearly show the historical emergence of Swahili identity and the growing distinction from Arab identity.

It was during the German colonisation that a new group emerged, distinct from Arabs and tribal groups, the Swahili group, identifying itself as the bearer of a new culture. During the pre-colonial and pre-Arab eras, the city was built around its fish market. Then came the slave trade and Islam: the Arab caravans arrived, and with them the detribalisation of groups settling in town. Under German colonisation the railway and Christianity appeared, and the group of Islamized Bantu, the Waswahili, emerged. The process continued under the British and the Waswahili gained importance. Foreigners arrived in great numbers with Independence.

The local tribal groups opposed the Arabs, while the Waswahili became the mobile group assimilating the newcomers according to their way of life. In short, the Arabs were not born Swahili, even if they were the first to speak Kiswahili. Their tribe is different. The disjunction between language and ethnic identity is the original characteristic of Tanzania and consitutes, to my mind, the fundamental structure on which Ebrahim Hussein's oeuvre is built - and permits the understanding thereof. It allows the Mwarabu (Arab), coming from the Muslim community, Ebrahim Hussein, to identify with the myth of 'Swahiliness', the incarnation of the myth of Independence, carried forward by Mwalimu Nyerere, a Catholic from the Great Lakes. The Mswahili, a zealous servant of Arab and, later, colonial authority, became the vehicle for the myth of Independence and socialism, signified by the word *Azimio* - declaration.

Swahiliness, the bearer of a practical, international lingua franca, was then adorned with ideal qualities for the formulation of an ideology of national liberation, social integration and development necessary for the legitimization of the post-colonial political power (Constantin, 1986:251).

In short, the post-colonial political power brought the Kiswahili speakers, and among them the Arabs who wished it, a new political identity, by turning the language of the coast into the language of the country. Only, this political identity was tributary to the vicissitudes of political power and, eventually, to the failure of the socialist plan, through weak-willed and contradictory orientations (Hartman, 1987) which wearied its own defenders, and caused, to a great extent, the identity crisis illustrated in Ebrahim Hussein's plays.

The ethnic identity was never a linguistic identity: this Swahili originality is an extraordinary asset for the construction of a national state and culture. The message of the water spirit is truly to exploit Kiswahili to unify the tribes; and Kinjeketile is the medium of this message, even if he has doubts about the means through which to bring it about.

The independence in Tanganyika and revolution in Zanzibar imposed Kiswahili as the national language with the former pursuing the goal of building socialism. Will the different ethnic groups and the different social classes gradually merge inside the national melting pot? Will new divisions start appearing? *Mashetani* describes the apparition of these new divisions and the doubts they give rise to within the young intellectual generations. The following two plays show us the return of the identity question seen through the political crisis. *Arusi* shows us a Swahili culture of ceremony, without any hold on the economic and political reality. Finally, *Kwenye Ukingo wa Thim*, expresses the triumph of Kiswahili, a truly international language capable of describing the condition of the Luo and Gikuyu of Nairobi. It is also the admission of the failure of the dream of the fusion of the ethnic groups within a national melting-pot, a dream which Hussein shared with the great Kenyan writer Ngugi.

Savage capitalism destroyed the coast; tribalism undermined the interior. *Ukabaila* (class exploitation) and *ukabila* (tribalism) are still there. The question is no longer to unify Kiswahili speakers in order to mould them into a nation (feudalism, landlordism, *u-mwinyi*), that has been settled in Tanzania, even if this nation and this power are threatened with failure.

Today, Ebrahim Hussein asks himself in Kiswahili who he is. It is in Kiswahili that the tragedy of human existence is revealed. The success of the socialist power has been to allow this question on identity to be posed in Kiswahili.

6
Sheikh Ebrahim, Actor and Martyr

Kwani suala sio kusema au kutokusema..., suala ni kufumba.
(Hussein, *"Ngugi: Ugumu wa ukweli anaosema"*, Zinduko No.3, 1978, 36, cited in Philipson, 1989:237).

For the question is not to tell or not to tell, the question is to disguise... (*kufumba* from *fumbo*: "mystery, enigma, veiled language, obscure words, a conversation in a language foreign to someone; to speak enigmatically, allegorically, to veil one's language..." Sacleux, *Dictionnaire Swahili - Français*)

In his essay on Jean Genet, Jean-Paul Sartre quotes the following remark by T.E. Lawrence:

"And then madness was very near as I believe it would be near the man who could see things through the veils at once of two customs, two educations, two environments. Such is the case of the traitor. Within the group he is the other, and the man through whom the group will know itself as another. But this is so because he is first, within himself, another than himself. The traitor is a madman, it is himself whom he betrays. A disintegrating society, an individual who is an enemy to himself and who experiences this disintegration as a disease of his personality: such are the necessary and sufficient conditions for betrayal to occur (Sartre, 1963:174).

The analysis made by Sartre, his method of critical social psychology, highly informed about the political and social framework within which the literary plan unfolds, may suggest a few useful trails for him who, in Tanzania and in the Swahili world has rather become the Ebrahim case. A respected author and professor, he has been, as we know, jobless for ten years and today lives alone in his father's house in Dar. For many, he has disappeared from the literary scene. Luckily this is not the case, but there is, in his present attitude, in this type of self-imposed reclusion, a form of challenge. Ebrahim is an actor making himself into a martyr.

What is he a martyr of, why does he keep himself apart. What does he want to tell us? I will search for the answer to this question in terms of *siri* (secret), *kitendawili* (enigma), and *mwiko* (taboo resting on a pact): terms around which Ebrahim Hussein's oeuvre gravitates and which introduce an element of mystery and obscurity into his oeuvre. The Sartrian question: "What is literature?" is still an issue in Africa, and particularly so with those who have chosen to write in an African language and who are far from being in the majority.

Two plays by Hussein - *Jogoo Kijijini* and *Ngao ya jadi* - are presented as enigmas. The term "secret" is often used in his last works as far as the term "pact" is concerned, it is a rather good account of the relationship between Kinjeketile and Kolelo, between the soothsayer and the local spirit...

The enigma: Jogoo Kijijini

The two dramatic monologues which went unnoticed in the seventies, *Jogoo Kijijini* and *Ngao ya Jadi* have not been translated and enjoy a deserved reputation of great obscurity.

> *Racconta due fiabe (ngao) rielaborandole pero a modo suo, in maniera molto sofisticata e per la verita quasi incomprensibile.* (Bertoncini:282).

> He tells two tales, revised in his own way, very sophisticated and almost incomprehensible.

An early sign of new readings: at the tenth conference on Swahili studies held in May 1997 in Bayreuth, Abdilatif Abdalla, the Kenyan Swahili poet, a respected professor and writer, chose these two plays by our writer to crown his reading of Swahili works. The public response to the storyteller, the participation of the audience, their laughter at times, showed convincingly that the texts were becoming readable, despite the challenge posed by their ornate language. The tale turns into an enigma after a theatrical dialogue that only the author has acted out.

Hussein is a great actor for those who have seen him act: Joachim Fiebach compares him to Dario Fo (1980:368). The poem that he was reciting, that he was acting, has become a reference in the history of Swahili poetry. It is, therefore, no longer strange to note the silence which has for a long time surrounded the two 1975 plays. Yet, these two monologues are dialogues: the public responds to the storyteller, taking up a refrain similar to the way in which he discreetly participated in the tale *Sultan Majnun* (Steere, 1870).

Mtambaji hadithi: Paukwa!
Kiitikio: Pakawa!
Mtambaji hadithi: Hapo kale palikuwa na Mkunazi (JK:13)

The storyteller: Paukwa!
Refrain: Pakawa!
The storyteller: Once upon a time there was a jujube-tree

The jujube-tree is that Oriental tree which, according to the ancient authors, had the power of making one forget one's country of birth... For some, it is the 'Lotus-eating' tree in Book IX of the Odyssey Book. A strange presence in a village we're about to discover, populated with invaders who have come from who knows where...

A creeper chokes the tree, and its death coincides with the arrival in the village of conquerors who divide the village into two parts. The only thing is that this invasion is presented by rather obscure images:

Kunazi zikakatika	The jujube-trees broke
Zao linatoweka	The fruit disappeared
Na ukafu ukazidi	And the drought has worsened
Jogoo anawika	The cock crows
Ni asubuhi	It's morning
Mbali ukingoni	Far away on the bank
Mboni ya juwa yachungulia jangwani	The eye of the sun looks at the desert
Mtu	A man
Nyayo kisogoni	His foot at the nape of his neck
Jicho ardhini	His eyes on the ground
Ulimi kinywani	His tongue in his mouth
Ukihesabu hatua za hatima	If you count the last steps

Baina ya unyayo	Between his feet
Karibu na sikio	Near his ear
Aushi na malalamiko	Incessant complaints
'Nyayo litamka	And his feet said
'Ewe sikio sikia;	Listen, ear, listen
Mimi mahabusi wa myaka	I'm a prisoner of the shoe
Wa k'yatu ulichonivika	That you put on me
Gizani ninadhoofika	I'm getting weak in the dark
Nataka ona juwa la	I want to see the sun of a
siku njema	Good day
Mimi mahabusi dhalili	I'm poor recluse
Mfungwa wa yako akili	Prisoner of your conscience
Akili nisiyo ikiri	Conscience I don't recognise
Wala nisiyo ikubali nafsia	Which deep in me I don't agree
Nimechoka thama 'mechoka	I'm tired, really tired
Najuwa Jogoo awika	I know the cock is crowing
Lakini mi nakwaruzika	As for me, I'm being bruised
Katika giza lisilo 'nufaiya	In useless darkness
Humu k'bandani kiyatuni	In my small shoe house
Naishi gizani tabuni	I live in darkness and misery
Nachunika mikwaruzoni	I am being torn by chafing
Ninapopambana na hii dunia	As I struggle against the world
'Kili yatuma mikonoyo	The spirit appeals to your hands
Kila hiyo kucha ijayo	Every day that breaks
'Subuhi ihudhuriayo	Every morning that arrives
Katika kiatu kunifungulia'	From the shoe to release me
Lakini sikio	However the ear
Lilikuwa sikio la kufa	Was destined to die
Hasha	No,
Aslani halikufa	It was not dead
Ingekuwa sikio limekufa	If it were dead
Singelewa upepo pitao njia.	I wouldn't understand
(JK:14)	The wind blowing across the way.

Man walks and suffers. His body, his feet complain, and a strange dissociation occurs within the hero: mind and body seem to be struggling. What's more, this concrete poetry (shoe, chafing, ear) is strange within the lyrical context of the complaint. Here we are touching on a brand-new aspect of Hussein's poetry: the mixture of genres, producing effects of detachment, de-automation of language, generating poetic effects, which Brecht would use as drama theory. It is clear that this form of expression, which has broken with metric and thematic conventions of represented poetry,(like *ngonjera*, for example), triggers a novel effect with Swahili readers, which increases the impression of the text's hermeticism. The choir then speaks, using a Swahili expression taken from Arabic (*Naam Twaib*: Yes, certainly).

Lakini	But
Siku ile	On that day,
Kaumu ilisimama	The crowd stopped
Ile vile	Like that
Au ya jogoo kulizana	Or the cocks to quarrel
"Vipi? Mbona kaipoteza sautie?"	Why, how has it lost its Voice?
Kiitikio: naam twaib	Refrain: Yes, certainly
Mtambaji hadithi:	Storyteller:
Ama juu ya mtu wetu	And about our man, I've
Kwamba	Already
Yeye alianguka	Said that he fell
Yeye aliseleleka	That he got stuck
Ye aliterezeka	That he slipped
Juu ya mgongo wa	On the back,
ki-Van Goghia (JK:19)	Van Ghogh-like.

The reference to the cursed painter of the last century is an allusion to the independence generation which our poet considers lost, despite its great dreams. We're in a work mixing registers and references: on the next page the young man becomes a type of *shaman*, and, at the same time, he yearns for purification in the Zam Zam river, the waters of Mecca...(JK: 20)

Si mbali pale alipoangukia	Not far from where he fell
Kijiji kilikuwa kinamngojea	A village was waiting for him
Lakini kwa vile	But because the hiccups had
Kikwiki kilivyomshika	Taken hold of him
Vile	As drought
Ukafu ulivyompata	Had gripped him and made
Na vile	Him
Kiu kilivyomkamata	Yearn for
Alitaraji maji ya zamzamia	The Zam Zam waters
Ndiyo hapo kijana	At that moment the young man
Mti'kaukamata	Grabbed a tree
'Kaukamata 'kaupinda	Grabbed it, twisted it,
'Kaupinda 'kaupanda	Twisted it, climbed it
Ka ' manati	And catapulted himself
Kijijini kairushia	Towards the village
Ilikuwa magharibi	It was dusk
Alipo fika	When he got there
Hakufikia uwani	He didn't fall in the courtyard
Bali alifikia barazani	But landed on the verandah
Ili	So
Mlango Mkuu kuupitia	As to enter through the main
(JK:20)	Door.

The young man falls right in the middle of a divided village.

Lakini ile njia iliotuleta	And this road
Ile njia tulioifuata	After bringing us here
Hiki kijiji kiliikata	Dropped us
Na kijiji	And then
Baadhi mbili zikatokea	It's here it disappeared
Na nd'o hapo	And that's how
Homa kijiji ikaingia	The fever entered the village
Ama ile duara tuliokuta	And the circle that we found
Zile nyingi sana kuta	So many walls
Lahaula,	My God, these things
haya hatukuzingatia	We had not foreseen

Wala wakati mwingi haukupita	It wasn't long after
Miti ya kitongoji tukaikata	We cut the village trees
Na mafundi wao tuwakamata	Took their artisans
Mlango wetu Mkuu kutuumbilia	To build our main door
Hatukujuwa asilani	But we never knew that
Kuwa ile nyumba thamani	That valuable house
ilijengwa kichuguuni	Was built on a termites' nest
Makao ya mchwa	The residence of the termites
'naowasikia	You hear people talk about
(JK:25)	

Finally they collapse, these houses with their beautiful, finely sculpted doors, so typical of the coast and of Zanzibari culture, and also of Kilwa. What *"the sad army of termites"*, as Christophe, the sovereign of another island in distress, calls them (Césaire, 1963:150), has not eaten, is demolished by a storm. Only an old woman remains to tell this story to a young man who becomes the sacrificial heifer in order to expiate the events he has just been told. The cock announces every day, and every new episode.

Uchwa shababi	The young termites
Watunza jadi	Guardians of traditions
Walo' ahidi	Who'd promised to protect
Kuhami kijiji na kukiangalia	and watch over the village
Siri hii	This secret
Hatukuijuwa mwanzoni	We didn't know at first
Kwani	Because
Macho 'likuwa utosini	Our eyes were looking back
Na viatu	And our shoes
Tukiviparaza njiani	We dragged on the road
Tope chafu, watu tukiwarushia	Throwing dirty mud at people.
JK: 26	

Lucidity comes, thanks to the young man. The villagers must look ahead; but a sacrifice, a tribute is also necessary.

Na ile njia	And that road
Baada kutuleta	After bringing us
Hapa ikatubwata	It dumped us
Halafu ndiyo hiyo	And there
Hapa kijijini 'kajiondokea	It went its way from the village
Pole pole ikapanda	Little by little it climbs
Pole pole ikatanda	Little by little it spreads
Juu ya mlima	Over the mountain
Karibu ya mawingu ikapotea	Near the clouds it disappeared
Ikapita milimani	It passed over mountains
'Katambaa mabondeni	Wound through the village
Ikajichovya mitoni	Plunged into rivers
Mpaka baharini	Up to the sea
Kule 'likotoka kjizamia	Drowned where it came from
(JK:26)	

The fluid construction of the narration, the association of images show that the text is first and foremost a poetic monologue, staged by the interventions of the choir, which curiously, to my knowledge, has only been represented by Hussein himself.

Interpreting the text poses a double problem: this fable is a political allegory. The author himself invites us to decipher the enigma he proposes; the text becomes a *kitendawili*, one of those genres of Bantu speech, a sort of riddle which lends itself to unfolding as a tale. The author places his show within the genre of oral literature, which he diverts by appropriating the formulas of fairytale beginnings and enigma endings. This mixture signals that we're very far from the folklorish respect for tradition.

Basi wewe msimulizi	So, you the storyteller
Basi wewe mwenye ujuzi	So you with the knowledge
Uliofanya upekuzi	You who did research
Tueleze mambo yakatueleya	Explain to us so that we May understand

Mtambaji hadithi:	Storyteller:
Ngojeni	Wait
kwanza kisa 'kumalizieni	First I have to finish this tale
Halafu	Then
Hizo hit'lafu hakikisheni	Be certain of the faults
Msifanyeni	Don't do anything
Mambo pupa bila ya kuzingatia	In a rush without thinking
Kiitikio: Naam, twaib	Refrain: Yes, certainly
(JK:29)	

For Fiebach (1993) the desire to experiment with new forms of drama by reinterpreting traditional modes of speech is a major trait of Hussein's oeuvre. In the Swahili oral tradition, when the public cannot solve the enigma, the riddle-teller asks to be given the 'title' of a city of his choice before revealing the meaning of the riddle. However, Ebrahim Hussein doesn't give the answer and leaves us in the dark.

Inaonekana kwamba	It appears that
Kwamba ililazimika fidia	That a tribute was required
Nd'o kijana, ng'ombe kajigeukia	So the young man became The sacrificial calf
Na vile	And as
Iliaminika pale	It was believed there
Kama ilivyoaminika kale	As it was in ancient times
Kwamba Musa	That Moses
Kutoka fufufu yule	By his death
Ni uhai mpya atawaletea	Would bring them a new life
Ama ule upenu wa awali	That original path
Ukageuka kuwa chano ali	Because a beautiful plate
Au kuwa sinia iliyo mali	Or became a valuable tray
Ng'ombe wa hakika kujichukulia	Bearing the true calf
Masikini kijana masikini	Poor young man
Masikini lahaula masikini	Poor, Oh God, poor
Haya yote yanajilia nini?	Why does all this happen
Hata ye kujifanya ng'ombe alia?	Even to turning oneself Into a sacrificial calf?

Swala hili muliloniuliza	The question you've
Hivi kwangu mimi ni miujiza	Asked for me it is a miracle
Basi hapa kadi tamati	So there I stop
Kadi tamati kalitamati	Here is the end
Maneno yamenisaliti	Words have betrayed me
Na kisa pia kimenikaukia	And the story has dried up
Kiitikio:	Refrain:
Kisa tumekisikia	We've heard the tale
Utungo 'metuelea	The composition is clear
Maneno 'metuingia	The words have entered us
Ama maana hatujaambulia	But we haven't understood

(JK:30)

We are far from the traditional enigma which is sometimes caught in the automatism of tonal riddles, the mechanisms of which have been well described by Clementine Faik-Nzuji. This speech is not socialised, nor recreational. It's poetic and prophetic; it wants to be interpreted. Performance rules require the storyteller to ask the public to nominate a city in order to conclude. Which cities are proposed? Kigoma, Dodoma, Dar es Salaam: the three compose a political geography of Tanzania, from Arab penetration to socialist affirmation.

A decade later, Lihamba and Fiebach propose their reading of this pioneering text. According to them, it reflects the revolution in Zanzibar, the country with beautiful, sculpted doors, in which the jujube tree quarter occupies the central square of the Old Town. In his heart of hearts, Ebrahim entered into rebellion against the righteous conformism of the admirers of the humanist and chaotic socialism of the Ujamaa whose Zanzibari version borrowed more from Castroism than from Scandinavian social democracy... With whom could one share one's reservations in the seventies?

There is one point they don't insist upon, and which seems to us of increasing importance in Ebrahim's work during those years: the theme of sacrifice. The *Sura* cow is sacrificed like the young man and, in a certain way, like the artist (Van Gogh) who commited suicide for his work. Numerous references (Van Gogh, Keats, the Koran) appear in a fairytale riddle, presented in scenic form. We are far from the other scenic dialogues of that period, like the *Ngonjera*.

Here we are invited to reflect on history and sacrifice. A reflection centred on a jujube tree and a city with tall gates... And the cities proposed by the public in answer to the storyteller's invitation, are not the one we thought: Zanzibar, the city of jujube trees and sculpted doors, already produced in *Mashetani*. There was even a young man who came from afar to bring this world down: it was the strange Okello, the leader of the raid on the police gun room which triggered the Zanzibar revolution (Lofchie, in *Cliffe*, 1975). An ephemeral field marshal, an authentic warlord, swept away by the storm he unleashed... A strange character, quickly forgotten, he is a mystical and unpredictable troublemaker of whom Ebrahim Hussein's young character (*kijana*) reminds me.

There is radical novelty in this work, as Fiebach rightly points out. Tradition has been turned around: genres are mixed, registers of expression are confused. European modernity is intertwined with Koranic references, the Swahili choir starts a dialogue with a shaman-like epic hero. And all of that is represented by the author, who himself became a sort of epic and lyrical Dario Fo... This makeshift modernity is eloquent. It is that of national culture, but here it is the reverse, the other face of it, the dark face, that which must be masked in order to speak. Ebrahim will be clearer in his other monologue, but he will not be heeded more...

Ngao ya Jadi (The Ancestors' Shield) works on the same principle of an enigma unfolding as a fairytale and a theatrical performance. It tells the story of a very old village (*kitongoji cha zamani*) which must sacrifice one virgin to the Sesota Serpent every year.

Kitongoji hiki kilikuwa	The village was
kinaitwa	called
Kitongoji -Masononi	The village of sadness
Kilikuwa na watoto	It had children
Watoto wazuri	Beautiful children
Na wenye nyingi shani	With many good qualities

Na kila	And everyone
Aliyewaona watoto Masononi	Who saw the children of Sadness
Moyo wake uliingiwa	His heart was filled
Gharba,	With wonder
Mapenzi	Love
na Imani	And faith
Miaka ikapita	The years passed,
Miaka ikapita	And passed,
Miaka ikapita...	And passed...
Watu wakaoana	People got married
Watu wakazaana	People were born
Na mali ikazidi	Prosperity grew
Lakini mioyoni	But a sadness was
Simanzi ikatambaa	Spreading into their hearts
Simanzi haini	Treacherous melancholy
Kwa kila mwana -Masononi	In each of the children of Sadness
Hatua si hatua	Not far from there
Ni mdomo na pua	As close as between the
Liliishi kitongojini	Mouth and the nose in a hamlet
Joka la vichwa sabini	lived the seventy-headed serpent
Na kila aliyeliona	And everyone who saw it
Joka hilo maluuni	That nasty serpent
Moyo yake 'liingiwa hofu	Was filled with fear
Na mashaka ya kiinsani	And human doubts in his heart
Miaka ikapita	The years passed
Miaka ikapita	And passed
Miaka ikapita	And passed
Simanzi ikatambazika	Melancholy spread
Huzuni ikatandazika	Sadness grew
Na majonzi yakazidi	And bitterness increased
Kwani	Because
'Likuwa tabia makini	It was an old custom
Kila mwaka ukibaini	That every year

Joka hushuka kijijini	The serpent descends on the village
Kuchukuwa mali na binti	To take away its booty and
mzuri mmoja	Beautiful young girl
Basi	Thus
Siku ya siku ikatimu	The day of days came
Jua ukungu 'kashtumu	The sun chased away the mist
Si m'amuma wala 'simamu	Neither the disciples nor
Wanakijiji wakajikutanilia	The Imam stayed behind
(NJ:34)	The villagers assembled

The village 'meeting' reaches the decision that an end must be put to the serpent, and an old, toothless woman makes the speech declaring war:

Huyu nyoka nduguzanguni	This serpent, my brothers,
Si nyoka wa hii mitini	is not a snake of these trees
Ajifichae majanini	who hides in the grass to strike
Kugonga apitae mmoya mmoya	those who pass, one after another
Huyu nyoka nduguzanguni	This serpent my brothers
Siyo nyoka wa chini duni	is not a crawling beast
Au yule nyoka wa majani	or that snake of the grass
Mwenye sumu 'lo hafifu	with weak and harmless
'sojipandia	poison
'Huyu nyoka na'ambieni	This serpent, I'm telling you,
Ni joka kubwa la zamani	is a great serpent of the past
Linavyo vichwa sabini	which has seventy heads
Na kila shingo yake lina lake koya	each with its own neck
'Enyi wangu sikilizeni	'You my people listen!
Sikilizeni tahadharini	listen and beware
Joka hili dudu hiyani	this serpent is a beast
Linatowa moto linapopumuwa	that blows fire when it breathes
'Ama	'Oh
Yafaa sana tumtafuteni	we have to look
Sisi wetu hapa mtemi	for a young leader amongst us

Kijana; wala siye mimi	and it will not be me
Atakae pambana na joka	who will fight with
pamoja	the serpent
'Ha nyie nakuambieni	I'm telling you
Tena ha ' nakuusieni	I'm pleading with you
Tafadhali nyi yapimeni	Weigh my words carefully
Musijesema nye sikuwaambia	Don't say I didn't tell you
Tena	Besides that
Kabla hi vita haijawa	Before leaving for war
Ama bora sana 'ngekuwa	It would be a good thing
Kumuambia bwana Tewa	To tell Tewa to take the
Ngao ya jadi,	Ancestors' shield
mtemi kumletea	To our champion
'Pia	Also
Mwambieni bwana Mkwawa	Tell Mkwawa that our spear
Mkuki wetu wa tangu Hawa	Coming from the time of Eve
Mbele ya watu hawa hawa	In front of these very people
Mtemi hapa lazima aje kupewa	To our chief it must be given
(NJ:38)	

The young leader, Mkwawa, bears the name of one of the heroes of the WaHehe revolts, almost a contemporary of Kinjeketile, famous in Tanzanian history. Against this serpent, he engages in a battle worthy of the great epics of Central Africa. The fight begins in challenge mode: an ancient genre of Swahili speech, and continues in possession mode. The text is mixed with memories of the time of Eve, taken from the Koran, and with praises of the hero...

Mkwawa is possessed by the spirits of the ancestors. He certainly succeeds in cutting off one of the heads, but this beast is a hydra, and the heads grow again... Up to now they are still growing again, Ebrahim told me (in September 1995), while showing me a clipping from a paper denouncing child labour in the diamond mines of socialist Tanzania in the Nineties. The mine was the new chthonic monster...

Kijana mkuki chini kaukita	The young man held the
Kaukita	spear straight
Lile joka Sesota 'kaliita	He called Sesota the serpent
Akaliita	He called it
Akaliita	called it
Tena Akaliita	and called it
Lakini Sesota kimya hakuitikia	but Sesota did not answer
Mtemi akaanza kuranda	The *Mtemi* began a war dance
Mkuki chini 'nda	Raised the spear and
ukadinda	Struck the ground
Na ume'we ukampanda	His bravery increased
'Kitafuta mahali	Looking for the place
Pakujichomea	Where he'd pierce
Basi miujiza si hiyo	How wonderful
Ile ngao 'likuwa nayo	This shield he had
'Rusha kidaka kwa mayoyo	He threw it up into the air
Kama mtu na Ruhani	While shrieking like a man
aliyejiwa	Possessed by the devil
Huku atanda	Here he rises
Huku aranda	Here he strides
Huku adanda	He wanders,
Pale kama mpira	he climbs trees
akajinyambukia	Like a bouncing ball
Mahaba na kitongojize	The affection of the village
Na radhi za wote wazee	The blessings of the ancestors
Pia mapenzi ya nduguze	And the love of his relatives
Yalifanya nia na mwili kitu	Turned body and intention
kimoja	Into the same thing
(NJ:39)	

The fight against the serpent is a cosmic combat, taking place in the heavens, in which trees and lightning are the allies of the hero... But Hussein doesn't want us to get too carried away by the epic tale; he is also a follower of distance. This is only a story, a fairytale:

Lahaula masikini	We Poor things
Vita vya Wakuu	in what way do the wars of
Watoto vinahusu nini?	the ancestors concern the children?
Vita vya wakuu	In what way do the wars of the
Watoto au paka vinahusu	Ancestors concern the children
nini?	or cats?
(NJ : 41)	

And further on, he repeats this refrain while completing it, after the burning breath of the serpent which roasts everything that approaches it, people as well as children and cats.

"Vita vya Wakuu	In what ways do the wars of
Watoto au paka vinahusu	The ancestors concern the
nini?"	Children or the cats?
(NJ:41)	

A strange detail, a wink from the storyteller-actor to the audience, a rare example of humour in this text, this apparition of cats, these animals to whom we give our tongue, when riddles escape us, while the Waswahili call out names of cities...(translator's note: *donner sa langue au chat*, to give one's tongue to the cat, means to give in)

Lakini tuendelee na ngano	But let us continue our
Yetu...	tale...
Shaaban Robert	Shaaban Robert comes into
Uwanjani 'kajikita	the arena
Mathias Mnyampala	Mathias Mnyampala
Swahibuye 'kamwita	his friend calls him
Kezilahabi, Muyaka	Kezilahabi Muyaka
Wote wakaitika	They all answer
Watu nd'o kwa ngonjera	And the people get drunk
wakajileweya	on *Ngonjera*
(NJ:43)	

The disguises drop: suddenly, we're no longer in the fairytale, but in Tanzania's political history, and that of the Swahili language. Here, Ebrahim Hussein proposes a genealogy of his writing. Shaaban Robert is the inventor of modern Swahili prose; he is also the biographer of the queen of *taarab*, Siti Binti Saad.

The *Ngonjera*, as we know it, is the type of poetry created by Mnyampala, which became the official poetry of the Tanzanian regime, a type of poetry that Hussein is trying to get away from with his monologue in fairytale form.

Muyaka was the Swahili poet from Mombasa. He was free with regard to those in power, and to conventions. He is the emblem of the new poetical writing. Ebrahim Hussein published his first poem in the first comprehensive study on the people's poet from Mombasa: 'Muyaka, 19th Century Swahili Popular Poetry' (*Abdulaziz, 1979*).

Lastly, Kezilahabi is the great modern Swahili novelist, and a poet, another inventor of Swahili free verse, and, often, a perceptive critic of Tanzanian political culture.

Watu nd'o kwa ngonjera wakajileweya	All felt drunk with poetry
Na akina hohehahe hawa	all those pathetic individuals
Kabwela kina Huseni hawa	like these Husseins (myself)
Na'o mashetani wakajiwa	were in a trance
Wakapungwa na madadi wakaingiwa	possessed by demons
"Lakini moyoni	But sadness was slipping
Simanzi ikatambaa	into their hearts
Simanzi haini	A treacherous melancholy
Iliingia kifua cha mtemi	Entered the Mtemi's breast
Akafahamu	He understood
Tena akafahamu	And he understood
Sheria ngumu	the hard law
Hasa kwa moyo uliyekuwa huria	especially for a heart which was free
Kwamba	That
Kwamba kila mpiganaji idhilali	That every freedom-fighter
Yeye pia lazima huwa mdhili	Must himself become an oppressor

Wale anzali nao wahuni	All the proletarians and all the
Wakaja tuvalia miwani	Poor veiled their eyes
Meusi tena kubwa uso	With big sunglasses
Na bivyo nyuso kwa wao	So their faces would be hidden
'kajifichia	To themselves
Na sisi kina Pambo	And we Pambos
Tukaja zusha mambo	Came to add to the problems
Tukafanya urembo	We prettied ourselves
Magamba ya Joka tukajivalia	Sporting the serpent's skin
Na rafiki wa mtemi	And the leader's friends became
Wakawa stadi wa uchumi	great experts In economics
Bi Mwema kamtia mbaroni	The good lady trapped him
Yasmini	And they rubbed their hands
Mikononi mwao kajifirigisia"	With jasmine.
(NJ:46)	

Suddenly, the tone of the fairytale changes: it is no longer a time for humour, but for tragic lucidity. The heads of the hydra will always grow again. The seed of oppression is in the heart of man. The epic, the grandiose struggle between hero and monster, is followed by a reflection of bitter lyricism on our condition.

As André Jolles (1972:110) says: "The riddle is amplified until it becomes a narration which is, in a sense, a commentary on itself". What is numbered or coded in this social performance of the enigma is the secret of dissidence, which begins and protects itself through acting. It also has references: Pambo, the nouveau riche is the hero of a play by Penina Mlama Muhando (1975).

As for those donning the 'serpent's skin', they also appear in Kezilahabi's novel bearing that very name, *Gamba la Nyoka* (1979), *The Serpent's Skin*.

"*Maneno 'metuingia*	The words have entered us
Ama maana hatujaambulia"	And yet, their meaning escapes
(NJ:49)	us.

Hussein – jester/actor - proposes luminous enigmas no one wants to hear. He says what everyone knows, but what no one wants to talk about publicly. The enigma is a sort of insurance against the consequences of this dissidence, even if political violence in mainland Tanzania has never been as in neighbouring countries... Basically, he wore a mask to say what was nothing more than an open secret, namely, that the regime was already in crisis twenty years ago.

The *fumbo* is an aesthetic of disguise, producing a text of radical novelty in Swahili literature: a poetical monologue with a choir containing moments of great lyricism and narratives of epic combats. The author doesn't let himself be carried away by emotion: he watches over his narrative, and incessantly brings us back to it. He goes from the register marked by the Koran to epic rhetoric, from cosmic combats to social satire, from social satire to lyrical meditation on the human condition and the tragic feeling of life, the permanence of evil within us.

Ebrahim Hussein, one of the pioneers of the free verse in Kiswahili, is also the inventor of a type of genre mixing which is probably very disconcerting for listeners or readers. This *melange* operates by means of allusions (to personalities and situations) with frequent recourse to ellipsis which, in free verse form, keeps its incantatory rhythm created by frequent euphonies - a musical effect desired by a poet whose foremost pursuit in composition is of a musical nature.

Hussein knows Swahili metrics, but doesn't use it; he has broken with ready-made formulas. Writing free verse means rejecting several centuries of Islamic, Arabic tradition. What he has to say obeys an interior voice which has its own *"cante hondo"* - as Marguerite Yourcenar says about the Negro spiritual: *"The rhythm is within it, rather than it obeying the rhythm"* (Yourcenar, 1980:191).

Strange lucidity coming from an author acclaimed for his epic theatre and, particularly, for the play *Kinjeketile,* the intrigue of which, as we know, rests on a mysterious pact, surrounded by a taboo (*mwiko*) which the hero makes with Kolelo, the local god. A pact sets supernatural forces in action and seals an alliance, while a secret remains personal. To conquer the colonialists, a secret alliance must be sealed with the ancient gods. From this pact the hero brings back the invulnerability which is supposed to guarantee the *Maji Maji* revolt its victory.

But what does he give in exchange? We are not told. The religious notion of 'blood-pact' studied in Dahomey by Hazoumé throws some light on the pact concluded by Kinjeketile with the earth spirits who will give him control over water and, thus, the power to overcome bullets.

As the guardian of the secret of the relationship with the spirits Hongo and Kolelo, he discovers that the secret is a fraud, and that the pact is useless. Could religion be only the product of the mists of our imagination? The conversation with the spirits occurs in a secret language and in a sort of trance. When he comes to his senses, Kinjeketile realises the consequenses of his pact and takes fright. How can a spirit who promises liberation announce submission to the Arabs of Zanzibar? Is this abdication the security offered to the local gods, or to other spirits? Kinjeketile is locked inside his hut, offering a sacrifice which is the conclusion of the pact, but he is alone in this undertaking.

A serpent tries to go and see what Kinjeketile is doing: the sacrifice is linked to water and fire. The religion of the local earth functions according to pacts concluded in a secret language, in a moment of trance. However, this way of doing things will be challenged by the hero, who has regained his senses and who has caught a glimpse of his delirium. The alliance with the local gods may be only fraud, but it is necessary fraud to mobilise the fighters...

In the play bearing their name, the spirits, the *Mshetani*, have top billing and the secret is revealed in broad daylight. For the first time, the term is largely used, and gives rise to discussions. The whole first scene evolves around the secret of the spirit and its unveiling to a man who will allow him to take place of the *Shetani*.

Leo unatumia siri hii (MA:6)
Today you use this secret

"*Rafiki mpenizi, nina siri nataka nikuambie, nikupe. Lakini siri hii ni mimi. Mtu anayejua siri hii amenijua mimi. Na mimi moyo wangu unanituma nikufanye wewe hidaya wa siri hii...*" (MA:3)

My dear friend, I've got a secret I want to tell you, to give to you, but my secret is myself; the man who knows my secret knows me. My heart directs me to give you this secret...

Ukosefu wangu ni kukupa siri hii (MA: 3)
My weakness consists in giving you this secret

What is this *siri*, the spirit, the *Shetani's* secret? As in *Kinjeketile*, a word, given in the language of the spirits: in short, a new enigma... Several reading guides to his works have been published. His books are often prescribed in Kenya, according to the director of Oxford University Press whom I met in Nairobi in September 1995; and he has probably sold almost a million books. I was able to consult two commentary booklets on *Mashetani* where pupils had to answer the question: What is this secret?

Sengo, Kiango: *Siri hii ni elimu ambayo mkoloni alimfundisha mtawaliwa ili aweze kumtawala* (1975: 4).

The secret is the education given to a colonised person by a colonialist who thus has better control over him.

"*Siri hii ni mwenendo na utamaduni wake*" (Ikambili, 1992:5).
This secret is one's behavior and one's culture.

Hapo raia walipewa siri ambayo hasa ni elimu walitegemea tu ile siri ya mkoloni ambayo hawakujua ilikuwa imekusudiwa kumfaidi mkoloni (Kingei, 1987:6).

The masses received the secret, whih in fact was education, and the people became dependent on the colonialist's secret, without knowing that it had only been entrusted to them for the colonialist's advantage.

The commentary booklets published recently in Nairobi take up *ad nauseam* the themes tackled by critics during the previous years. For university and school critics, the secret assuring the colonialist of power over the colonised people, is education: the culture he transmitted and which keeps those he dominates at a distance. The secret is not a personal matter, but a political and social one, the interpretation of which is a matter of rather simple hermeneutics.

Brochures sold on the sidewalks of Dar es Salaam promise the secret of happiness; here the commentators reveal to us the secret of power and the cause of all Africa's ills. This is a strange rejection of education by educators: yet it takes on meaning here because it is done in Kiswahili.

We are not used to an African debate held in an African language. Thus we have access to an internal debate, the means of expression of which is not in contradiction with the contents – as is too often the case, for example, in the denunciations, in French of neocolonialism. Hussein's metaphysical ambition is here reduced to slogans, but slogans that are widely diffused.

In *Arusi* the term 'secret' once again appears. The context is totally different. It's the story of a marriage which fails, told in poetic language. *"Love knows no secret"* says a Swahili poem taken up in an anthology of great themes of love-poetry from the coastal region (Knappert, 1972:80):

Pendo halijui siri	Love knows no secret
Likifichwa hufichuka	When it is hidden it surfaces
Pendo halina hiyari	Love has no choice
Mtu linapomshika	When it seizes a man
Kila jambo atakiri	He will confess to everything
Jambo lisilofanyika	Everything that should not have been done

As if in answer to this poem on destructive passion, Hussein proposes his version of the relationship between love and secrets:

"Mapenzi, somo yangu, hayataki bayana; yanataka siri. Maisha usifanye kuyadhihirisha" (AR:11)

Love, dear comrade, wants to be hidden; it doesn't like broad daylight. Don't display your life in broad daylight...

The heroine Mwanaheri, abandoned by her husband, loves another man. The world of the village is a world where everybody knows everybody else, but love is an intimate, secret place. We are no longer looking for the secret of power but, on the contrary, we are in the sanctuary of secretiveness.

Hussein's art seems to have distanced itself from politics to bring us a play on marriage and its failure. The characters are no longer allegories of colonisation or of Africa; they are no longer possessed by spirits but, on the contrary, they try to live a lyrical existence in a world which is not lyrical at all. This tragic vision of poetry will triumph over the illusions of youth: everything will be known, and Mwanaheri was only dreaming... As the heroine's lover says:

"Nimpendae	The woman I love
Ana sura mbili	has two faces
Na haiba	The beauty on
Huwa midomoni	her opened lips
Iliyo benuka	is fringed
Katika kicheko	with inaudible
Nisichokisikia" (AR:19)	laughter

We have moved far away from the allegorical and political interpretations mentioned in the previous chapter.

The last published play, *Kwenye Ukingo wa Thim*, 'At the edge of the Thim,' - that no man's land of the dead for the Luo people - is placed entirely under the sign of the notion of retribution: Chira. What we did in the past pursues us, like the *furies*, and we will not escape punishment for our mistakes... But what do we know about the mistakes of others?

Why does the marriage between the Gikuyu barrister and the former *Mau Mau* militant end in this painful conflict over the husband's body and, finally, in the widow's death? Several clues suggest a secret, even more than one secret. Didn't the barrister have a mistress, and if so, shouldn't his role as good Christian be reviewed? He left no will, leaving his widow defenceless. Finally, didn't the latter betray the secret of the *Mau Mau?*

The pact notion is found once again in the *Mau Mau* movement, and remains centred in the religions of the earth. The heroine, Martha, is a former *Mau Mau* fighter, and she will not have recourse to the forces she could mobilise. Only her brother Ben has a secret to hide...

All the past actions are suggested in the play as possible causes for the punishments that rain down on the characters. All these secrets, everything the characters tried to push away from them, or even suppress, return with a vengeance - and explain the unleashing of the forces of death, if we accept what Ebrahim Hussein tells us in the introduction. The characters are no longer possessed: they are no longer allegories, but figurations taken from the contemporary world.

The last play takes us back to realistic theatre, steeped in poetical reflection on the relationships between human beings, their land, their religions. In it, the individual acquires a new poetical as well as psychological depth, far removed from the epic *Kinjeketile*. The world is overrun with tragic forces. The gods want to avenge themselves on men. This terrible return of the forces of tradition is a sombre reminder of lucidity: let us remember that it was, in a word, inspired by an incident...

Hussein uses the full keyboard of secrets to play his inseparable, political and personal breakdowns: in terms of the pact, the enigma, the hidden fault, the lovers' secret. A protean motive, the secret is also the oeuvre's deep driving force. It has to be understood as a mask, as a disguise. Those are the conditions for the secret to become the guarantee of the autonomy of the individual process, whether it be political reflection, amorous desire, or the spiritual quest of a person grappling with customs, with different types of education, different backgrounds. Is that the way to defend oneself against the madness glimpsed by T.E. Lawrence?

The secret explains types of behaviour having meaning only in a given social milieu and history. Writing is where the meaning of these types of behaviour can be read. Interpretation cannot stop at a simplistic sociology of literature in which there would be a secret of power or of success, or a secret of love as popular Swahili literature would make us believe. Ebrahim Hussein wants to expiate a betrayal for which nobody is blaming him. His secret is probably that he no longer believes in anything but literature, while, in his family and his world, one has, first, to believe in God; if possible in socialism; and, failing that, in money. Bad Muslim, bad socialist, bad capitalist... He hides, but there is a sort of game there.

At the same time, he bears witness to another literary requirement. He is truly a martyr of literature: his marginalisation is turned into theatre. His secret, which is still shameful, but well staged, is that, at the bottom of his heart, he no longer believes in anything other than poetry. It is an open secret, certainly, but one which exposes him to many inconveniences everywhere and, maybe even more, in the new African language literature of one of the poorest states in the world.

7
Between the Sea and the Walls ...

Naipenda fikira	I like an idea
Iliyojaa	That is full
Pana kama bahari	Wide as the sea
Nikiogelea	Whether I swim
Au nikipaa	Or fly,
Mwishowe si dhahiri.	I don't see where it ends.
Fikira nyembamba	A narrow thought
Huhadaa,	deceives us,
Huwa tasi la akili,	It dries up our mind
Na utu	And humanism is kept
Mahali duni huuweka.	In an inferior place.
(AR: 1980:9)	

Ebrahim Hussein is a poet, but he didn't publish a collection of his texts, only a few poems dispersed throughout different works. During each of my visits, he gave me some texts. His plays - notably *Jogoo Kijijini* and *Arusi* - are written in a free verse which extends the research on the liberation of Swahili poetry of which Kezilahabi's work, *Kichomi* (1984, translated into Italian by Elena Bertoncini) is a first version.

Between the ocean of ideas in which The Little Black Fish (*Samaki Mdogo Mweusi*, 1980) throws itself and the walls - including those of Berlin - which enclosed him his whole life, his poetry is that of a human being with a passion for freedom, who invents a new way of being a Swahili in Kiswahili.

Ebrahim Hussein was a militant student of TANU, Nyerere's nationalist party. His grandfather on his mother's side supported TANU in the coastal region. Ebrahim was also one of the students who left for the villages in the Usambara region, where he spent more than a year during the sixties. At the university he studied drama with professor Fiebach from East Germany; he was also the assistant of Wilfred Whiteley, the founder of Modern Swahili Studies.

While a student, he was already known as a poet and an actor. His poem *Ngoma na Vailini* (Drum versus Violin), dating from 1968, the year he was a student of Drama and Linguistics, was *"mimed by the author during a scenic representation"* (Abdulaziz, 1979:104). This text has become an obligatory reference when describing cultural conflict. As Bertoncini says in her reference work on Swahili literature, it is one of the *"most remarkable modern poems"* in which the author represents *"his inner conflict in symbolical terms: the violent and sensual beating of the drums, and the sweet and peaceful sound of the violin ..."*, but the poet *"doesn't risk choosing between the two"* (Bertoncini, 1985:22).

Ngoma na Vailini (1968)

Huo, huo mpwitopwito wa ngoma
Unachemsha damu yangu na matamanio yaliyo ladha
Damu iliyopozwa na kubembelezwa
Na vailini nyororo, vailini inayonita
kwa huzuni yenye furaha

Sasa nachemka na kupwitapwita
Sasa nna furaha na kuburudika
Mdundo wa maisha
Raha ya nafsi
Wapi niende?

Lazima ni-swali, lazima niabudu
Nimuabudu Allah
Lakini ataisikia sauti yenye panda
Sauti inayotokana na mwenye kuvaa
Kanzu na msalaba?

Drums versus the Violin

There it is, the beating of the drum
Making my blood pulsate with pleasurable desire

Blood that has been stilled and tamed
With the sweet violin, calling me, pleading with me
With sad mixed with joy

Now I am throbbing and vibrating,
Now I am soothed and calmed.
The pulse of life
The quiet pleasure of the mind
Which way shall I turn?

I should pray, I should worship God
I pray to Allah
But can he listen to a divided voice
The voice of one who wears both the *Kanzu* and the Cross?
(Hussein in Abdulaziz, 1979:105)

As the first Tanzanian professor of drama, Ebrahim Hussein collaborated with the entire new generation of Tanzanian writers and, particularly, his future colleagues, Penina Mlama and Amandina Lihamba. In 1986, he resigned from the university; he survived on translation assignments the Goethe Institute procured for him. He refuses to touch his royalties, available in Nairobi, his plays have been prescribed uninterruptedly for Kiswahili examinations in Kenya.

In 1990 he was briefly arrested and beaten by the Kenyan police for having offended the chief of State: he had thrown a chair at the portrait of the President which decorated the cafeteria of Nairobi University, which had just offered him a teaching post. Since then, the doors of the Kenyan universities where his books are studied have been closed to him. His solitude, which is timid and shy at the same time, has given him the reputation of being an intellectual poet difficult to get along with. He had few friends and in fact, led a very solitary existence, punctuated by visits to the Goethe Institute in Dar and to the Alliance Francáise where he reads the international press.

The Little Black Fish

Hussein's only non-dramatic texts are his rare poems and his translation of a text by the Iranian writer, Samad Behrangi. One may question the relevance of this translation being included in his works. The changes he made in the original work, his preface and the numerous resemblances we observe between this work and the rest of his oeuvre, leads us to think that the translator has appropriated the work of his predecessor.

Samad Behrangi (1939-1968) died a mysterious death; he was probably murdered by the Shah's secret police. He was a communist and his work, which was forbidden, circulated widely in Iran during the years preceding the Revolution of the Mullahs. It is still impossible to find. There are English translations in existence (I will use the one published in the United States in 1976), as well as an unpublished Italian translation. As I write this, a French translation has just been published (Chardon Bleu, 1997).

Hussein's preface is a four page text, dense and obscure, which ressembles a statement of a philosophical stand rather than an introduction to a children's book. Ebrahim himself is conscious of this and pointed out to me that the text was obviously incongruous at this point. Actually, everything is strange in this book: the translator's name is presented in the same character types as that of the author; although the text is presented as a translation, we are not told from which language. In his introduction, Hussein explains why he felt affected by this text:

"Fairytales of fear dominate the world" he tells us, and this fairytale describes fear. Nature and the environment scare him... Only:

> *All fairytales have an ending, even fairytales of fear... And the ending of this fairytale is not when the little fish cuts open a seagull's stomach, but when she is lied to and decides to discover the world. So something ordinary happens: she gets to know herself, herself and her society - new knowledge, a new education, freedom, total freedom to go for walks, to know other things, to feel the sun's caress giving new strength. The fear which was like a lump in her heart is like melting ice. She feels free... Once the mind has tasted freedom, it can no longer accept servitude. It is therefore not surprising that Behrangi, who had tasted this freedom of the little black fish chose to put his mind at peace and sacrificed himself for the happiness of the Iranians* (p.vii).

The Little Black Fish, *like Samad Behrangi, accepts to sacrifice himself for his brothers for all the other little fish* (p. viii).

Terror (*hofu*) and fear (*woga*) are vanquished by sacrifice (*muhanga*). In a sombre and threatening world a few prophets who are poets, open roads to light and to liberty. What's more, as he tells us in another preface, the world is sombre because the weight of personal - or collective - mistakes continues to weigh down on individuals. Such is the meaning of his *Chira* concept.

The world in which the fish lives is delimited by the torrent and the mountains: freedom is where the sea is. Here one finds once again the poetical geography feeding a part of East African theatre and structuring Hussein's universe: the mountain is opposed to the coast in the first play: the continent is opposed to the coast and to the islands. The heron has become a seagull.

The fish is the snail's friend, the foreigner putting ideas of liberty in his head. The fish is a girl: the mother fish's neighbours are the same type of busybodies we met in *Wakati ukuta* and *Arusi*. The world of the neighbourhood, of the family, is also the world of prejudice and of hostility towards foreigners, everything Hussein abhors... Our fish makes her own decision to leave. She must struggle against her stupid friends. She is sensible enough to follow the advice of the lizard who gives her a dagger for self-defence. She'll have the chance to use it against the pelican and the seagull. Tatu believes she can win freedom, but is cheated by her lover. Mwanaheri dreams about winning her freedom: these two plays are chronicles of defeat. Here our girl fish frees herself from all oppression, and first from that of the family and the village. Our fish talks to nature: it's the moon that tells her the truth about the river's course, while the other fish don't know anything about the world in which they live...

> *The fragrance of the mountain prairies filled the air and mixed with that of the waters. The little fish came to a place where the valley broadened and where the torrent billowed past. A new waterfall filled our fish with pleasure. She saw numerous fish. In fact, it was the first time since she had left home that she saw fish. The other little fish assembled and surrounded her.*
>
> *You're a stranger, aren't you?*
> *She answered: Yes, I'm a stranger here, I come from far away.*

Where do you want to go? one of the little fish in the group asked her.
I want to go to the end of this stream, answered the little fish.
Which stream? they asked.
Obviously the one we're swimming in, she answered.
And all the little fish said: But for us it's a river!
Our little, black fish said nothing.
One of the little fish said: Do you know the pelican's on your trail?
I know.

And that he's got a big pouch? they asked all together
The little fish answered: I know that too!
Another little fish asked her: You know all that and you still want to carry on?
Yes, she says, whatever happens, I have to carry on!

The rumour quickly spread in the region, amongst all the fish that there was a little fish who came from far away, who wanted to go to the end of the river, who wasn't afraid of anything, not even of the pelican. A few little fish wanted very much to go away with her. But they kept quiet for fear of the elders...

(Behrangi-Hussein, 1981:27-28)

She enjoys the sun's caress and learns that men have gone to the moon; men can do anything, if they unite. Here one recognizes Behrangi's universalist and humanist message which Hussein takes over as his own, modifying the original text. The world of liberation is the world of water and sky: it's not a world of landowners, although the fish admires the animals living with four feet on the ground... A meeting with a splendid antelope wounded by men gives us an opportunity to question a difference of detail:

In one place she saw an antelope hurriedly quenching its thirst in the stream. Good morning, beautiful creature, why are you in such a hurry? she said loudly. The hunter is chasing after me, answered the antelope. Look: he has shot at me. The little fish couldn't see the wound, but the antelope's limping made her understand that something terrible (kitu cha kutisha - the French, English and Italian translations (direct from Persian) read: 'she was telling the truth...') had taken place. Elsewhere turtles were napping in the sun, and further away the sound of gunfire filled the valley (Behrangi-Hussein, 1981:25).

The English text indicates the sound of *partridges,* when in fact it is about cartridges. Did the translator inadvertently confuse c and p? In that case it would be a slip, but which brings us back to the violent world of landowners in which beautiful antelopes are pursued by hunters, where terrible things happen, where the truth becomes *kitu cha kutisha,* something terrible...

Another noteworthy change occurs in the narration's dénouement: our fish, the seagull's prisoner, finds a companion to share her bad fortune, a little fish who waits, trembling, to be thrown to the offspring of the fishing bird. This little fish is unable to react and accepts its fate. Our female fish doesn't agree with this blind acceptance and shames her fellow fish who is dishonouring fishkind by his behaviour. She undertakes to cut an opening with her dagger in the seagull's skin in order to escape. But while the English text indicates that the fish takes it's chance when the slit is wide enough to slip through, the Swahili text clearly states that the female fish grabs the prisoner and throws him out, so that he has priority over the opening to freedom which she has made. The narration ends with this image: the escaped fish sees the seagull crashing to the ground, but doesn't see the female fish jumping into the sea. The female fish is lost, but her sacrifice has freed the other fish from a seagull... This slight change highlights sacrifice, a notion which Ebrahim Hussein returns to several times in the introduction.

We cannot avoid mentioning here that Persian themes have belonged to Swahili culture from the start, but that it's an area where mythology is probably mixed with a history which is still in the making. From the Shirazi of Zanzibar, who supposedly brought Islam to the islands, and maybe to the coast in the tenth century, to the Iranian revolution, which propagated another version of it which was revolutionary and tragic at the same time, the imagination of the poet, and the critic, is called upon. From the black colour, the duodeciman Shiites' favourite, which is that of the fish, to the tragic theme of the sacrifice of Imam Hussein, there is, in Iranian Shiism, elements of a tragic theatre which were noticed long ago, and which surround Hussein. We know that he belongs to the world of Sufi brotherhoods which are on the brink of orthodox Islam. The notion of an initiation voyage belongs to the tradition of Persian literature, especially to the famous twelfth century poem by Farid Uddin Attar, *Conference of the Birds*, the *Mantic Uttair*, of which Peter Brook gave a scenic version in 1979. Ebrahim Hussein's adaptation of Behrangi must be read against this poetical background.

> *The drama is possible only in Shiite Islam with its conception of Hussein's voluntary (though necessary) martyrdom and his fate as the skandalon which compels man to take sides for or against his imam, for or against his salvation. Thus orthodox Islam has not known the drama or the conflict depicting contradictory obligations in a man caught between several moral laws and its literature has refused to be concerned with conflicts that contrasting obligations, towards his own fate and toward his community on earth, have imposed on many a hero of the faith. The tortured conscience of the judge elect, on which history and anecdote have so much to tell, has never once been made the theme of literary treatment in our sense of the word* (Von Grunebaum, 1967:11).

Are these generalisations acceptable? I cannot speak on the philosophy of religions, only as a historian and critic of Hussein's oeuvre; it seems to me that Von Grunebaum's remark touches on a particular and central point of a specific oeuvre which "actualises and radicalises" subconscious cultural tendencies, to use Lucien Goldman's terms. Being the attentive and imaginative reader of Brecht he is, Hussein, like Peter Brook, is a poet translating myths and religions into dramatic language. He finds ample matter for cultural reinterpretation here.

The questions of liberty and sacrifice - tragic questions *par excellence*, questions that are central to our *Little Black Fish* adapted by Hussein - are not posed through an Iranian oeuvre by an author from Kilwa (a city of which the links with Shiism are testified by several documents), without touching the subtle and strong harmonics of Isamic culture. The *vailini* of the poem *Ngoma na vailini*, is that of the *taarab*, in which Iranian instruments, especially the *ud*, have an important place. At the end of the poem the author has to choose between the cross and the *kanzu*. Here the choice is also between orthodox Islam but also of ecstatic trance - his own - and Islam of tragic drama. The language of contemporary historical experience probably pushes Hussein towards a tragic world which he has difficulty expressing in the language of the norm and of ecstatic trance... The theatre, writing is where this tension is expressed, where the figures of liberation take shape, at the crossroads of many reinterpretations, new mixed figures of Swahiliness... And of a certain form of modernity which turns the mixture of shapes and questions into the sign of the freedom of art: these disrespectful connections are not those of the theologian, but of the artist.

> *How does one judge that the freedom of the novel - the invention of a writer who finds within himself a new resource of expression - is foreign to the liberties people would like to enjoy in social life? Could it not be that the dogmatism, which in the past was at the service of militant literature, is preserved in its reversal at the service of the literary work's autonomy? Rushdie's praise of interbreeding is not limited to the relations between men of different cultures or colour: it is also valid against the myth of the purity of literature...*
> *(Claude Lefort, 1994).*

Drama , as Hussein sees it, pertains to these questionings.

To be free...

It is difficult to meet with Ebrahim Hussein. Good luck, they told me, but the chances are you won't succeed! As with every trip, I found Ebrahim welcoming and available. His main activity is writing poetry. He entrusted one of his most recent texts to me, asking me to publish it, to show colleagues and readers that he continues working and creating...

Ukuta wa Berlin (1995)

Nilivyoota
Ndivo ilivyo kuwa
Jina la mfanyakazi, walichukuwa
Kujenga ufalme wao
Uso msingi, macho wala pua

Nilivyoota
Ndivo ilivokuwa
Muda haukuchukuwa
Ukuta ulianguka
Haukuwa na msingi
kiuno au muruwa

Nilivyoota
Ndivo ilivokuwa
Ulikuwa ukuta tu - mashine ya kuua
Rangi yake nyekundu
Ni damu ya vijana ilivyowaua

Furaha
Furaha ilikuwa
Kuona kuta zilizoshikana na kuta
Kuta kuiangukia kuta
Zisizo msingi, zisizo muruwa

Kuta
Zilikuwa kuta tu, mashine za kuua
Furaha kujuwa
Kuna muungwana
Mwenye hisi mwenye kujua

The Berlin Wall, 1995

I had a dream
It proved to be true
They had called themselves workers
To build a kingdom
Which had no foundations, eyes or nose

I had a dream
It proved to be true
In no time
The wall fell
It had no foundation, no back, no dignity

I had a dream
It proved to be true
It was only a wall - a killing machine
Red with the colour
Of the blood of the children it had killed

Joy
There was joy
To see walls linked to walls
walls pushing down other walls
Which had no foundation, no dignity

Walls
Which were only walls, killing machines
A joy to know
There was one who was
noble, sensitive, knowledgeable

The other city in which he had lived, this Berlin which he loved, has exploded and it is a good thing. He always had walls in his oeuvre, that of time, *Wakati Ukuta*, and then the Wall of Berlin. The *secular utopia* (to use John Paul II's expression), the dream, about the cruelty of which Hussein had no doubts, collapsed before our eyes. It was also a gigantic imposture, adorned with the blood of the workers. For a poet and a dramatist who experienced those years of *"war without battles"* (Heiner Muller) from the inside, this collapse has an extraordinary resonance. In his text he uses the words *muungwana, muruwa*: nobility, dignity, terms which are not very Brechtian at all. Terms which do not alienate and which refer back to a world of aristocratic values in which he takes part, in a sense, by his demand for freedom.

Hussein is alone in experiencing a poetical adventure in a world where he is of the opinion that there is no more room for poetry.

Everywhere walls surround the individual and they are not all made of concrete surmounted by barbed wire. He understands the reproach of individualism perfectly. Within a certain political perspective which, for him, dominates in Tanzania, there is no room for art: it has to be a weapon, or else a means of education. There is a *Sura* in the Koran about poets: *"as for the poets, they are followed by those who lose their way..."* (Koran, Sura 26). Hussein rather believes that he is the one showing the right way to go...

For him art has its laws, whether it be literature or sculpture. When he writes poetry, he first finds the form, then the rhythm, then the words come, but words are not primary. He has often told me how pleased he was to see his poem *Ngoma na Vailini* in print in Abdulaziz's classical work on Muyaka. He had presented it on stage with a montage of recordings. One day, during a stroll, he mimed to me the beginning of *Jogoo Kijijini*, his play written in free verse, just like *Arusi*. Since he reads French poetry and speaks French I told him that Rimbaud broke with regular metres; Ebrahim Hussein broke with the Arab metres of Swahili poetry.

Pierre Pachet's essay *Un a Un: de l'individualisme en Litérature* (One to One: On Individualism in Literature, Paris, 1993), may provide a grid for the understanding of Ebrahim's situation. Pachet deals with V.S. Naipaul, Salman Rushdie and Henri Michaux. The Africa in which Hussein grew up is the one which elicits the sarcasms of V.S. Naipaul. Naipaul's brother, Shiva, wrote some pages on Tanzania which are still topical.

His book *North of South* (1978) contains pages which are cruelly true about the Tanzania of the late seventies, the one Hussein left internally, in a sort of long, immobile drifting away. The scene of the interview between Shiva and the Tanzanian publishers says more than many theses about the intellectual climate of those years, and with a little imagination we can well picture Hussein's mute participation in this scene, while having our own thoughts on the matter. Shiva tells us that during his stay in Dar es Salaam at the end of 1977, he visited a Tanzanian publisher. He was received by three editors, amongst whom was the Swahili editor. The discussion was initially about his past work: *"Why do you not write about life on the sugar plantations?"*

he is asked. To which Shiva Naipaul can only reply that he doesn't know that life. His reward was to be categorized immediately as a member of the lower urban middle class. The whole 'dialogue' was marked, on the part of his Tanzanian interlocutors, by a condescending aggressiveness, expressed in the political cant of Marxism at its most simplistic; remember that these are the years of the famous Tanzanian debate.

Poor Shiva Naipaul is preached to about what he should write before being able to ask a question himself: *"What do you understand by development?"* The answer comes automatically: *"The building of a truly classless society, where each will give according to his ability and receive according to his need"*. These noble objectives do not seem sufficient for our incurable lower class bourgeois, who asks: *"What about the intellectual development of individuals who make up the society?"* 'Comrade' (*ndugu*, brother, was the official term) Moussa can find no other answer than: *"I do not understand what you mean by intellectual development? Is it another of your bourgeois notions?"* (Naipaul, 1978:282-283)

The reading of this scene of Tanzanian mores in the seventies enables us to understand the type of frustrations which Hussein must have felt. In fact, one finds, at the very core of Ebrahim's search, the quest for a truly interior liberty, one that would be guaranteed by the secrets of the spirits, or those of love. Soon after, in 1980, in another of his almost incomprehensible plays, on which Tanzanian reviews are scarce, *Arusi*, Hussein explains to us that his hero has the right to draw from the village community chest to help his parents - he is only taking what is owed him. Yet, this is a true episode of model village life, about a village in which he had lived. This key experience is narrated through the report of a documentary film crew:

After nine years, the village had no serious economic plan. The reason for the village not having a plan at this stage is that it had recently lost its long-standing leader. Until he left, it was he who usually made the plan. This was because he was an exceptionally intelligent and able man who had completed primary school. He had increased villagers' participation many times over during his time in office, but the village had not yet reached the stage where the plan was really made by the people and anchored in their minds. When he first took office, only a few villagers could read and write. Now most can.

The loss of this leader was sudden. It was partly caused by the citizenship issue. He became frustrated, disheartened and depressed. He fled the village, taking over Shs 3,000/= from village funds with him. Upon arriving home in Kenya, he wrote to the village, explaining where he was, what he was doing, and why he left the village (Cliffe et al, 1975:393).

To put it differently: how could this remarkable man have been broken by a system which was more chaotic than perverse, which allowed a village to be led by a militant to whom the Tanzanian state refused citizenship? This individual was indispensable. A strange fragility: he could not stay, and everything collapsed. It's the story Ebrahim Hussein tells us in his own way in *Arusi*. His hero wrote a letter of resignation:

Diwani: (anasoma barua)
Ndugu wanakijiji
mutapopata barua hii
mimi nitakuwa nisha kuwa ndani
kifungoni. Lakini hii si kitu,
kitu ni kwamba nyinyi wenzangu
muelewe kwa nini jambo hili
limetokea. Siku ile nilipotoka
hapo kijijini nikafika Tanga.
Nilipofika Tanga nilienda benki
na mambo yetu yalifanikiwa;
njiani nikaiona gari inayokwenda
Mombasa na kurudi siku hiyo hiyo.
Sijui ilikuaje nikajiona tu kuwa
nimeshaomba ruhusa na kuwa ni
abiria. Ilikuwa nia yangu kwenda
Mombasa kuwaona jamaa na kurudi.
Lakini nilipofika huko niliikuta
hali ya nyumbani mbaya sana.
Kwanza walikuwa wagonjwa, tena

*walikuwa wamo katika deni. Hiyo
nyumba yao, ambayo ni nyumba
wanayokaa na kupangisha ingeuzwa,
na wao ingewabidi kuishi barabarani.
Nikachukua fedha nikalipa deni hilo
ya Bwana Mzuri, mtu aliyekuwa anawadai.
Nikisema nilichukua fedha hiyo
ninamaanisha kuwa sikuiba;
maana mimi nimefanya kazi miaka
mingi katika Kijiji chetu
cha Ujamaa bila kupata malipo
yoyote. Kwa hiyo fedha hii
niliyochukua ni ijara ya kazi
niliyoifanya miaka kadha wa kadha.
Na nitaporudi baada ya kifungo,
nitahisabu kuwa nimechukua fedha
kiasi kadha hisabu yangu, Sina zaidi.*

Wenu,

Kahinja.
(AR: 44.45)

The councillor reads the letter:

My brother villagers, when you receive this letter, I will already be in prison. But that is not the issue. The problem is that I want you to know the cause of what happened. The day I left the village, I arrived in Tanga, went to the bank and everything went off well. On my way, I saw a bus doing the return trip to Mombasa on the same day. I don't know how it happened, but I realized that I had asked permission and that I was already travelling. My idea was to see my family and to come back. But when I arrived, I found them in a bad situation: first, they were ill, second, in debt. And if the debt was not paid, the house they were living in and (part of) which they were renting would be seized. They would be condemned to live in the street. I, therefore, took the money to pay this debt. When I say "took the money", I

would like to say that I didn't steal, because I worked several years in our Ujamaa village without ever being paid. Therefore, the money involved is salary for the work I did for many years. And when I return, after prison, I'll account for the money on the basis of what was due to me.
I have nothing more to add.

Yours,

Kahinja...

That is the letter Kahinja writes to the villagers. Hussein tries to understand the break that has occurred within his hero, the idealist who loved *"ideas that swell"*. The man expects to answer for his deeds, to try to justify them, to pay for them. Hussein puts value on dignity, *muruwa*. As Pachet observes concerning V.S. Naipaul's oeuvre, but it could also apply to Shiva and Hussein, who experience the same refusals:

> *"There is a modern anguish in the face of politics which is probably contemporaneous with modern democracy. It is especially felt in countries freeing themselves from colonisation, impoverished countries, the elite of which had to suffer the psychological ordeal of dependence on an admired and envied metropolis. Becoming truly independent in these conditions is incomparably more difficult than to allow oneself to be lulled by the justifying ideology which turns one into an eternal victim and accumulates on the former coloniser, on the slave-trader, on the racist the totality of the error"* (Pachet, 1993: 107).

Hussein's poetic theatre is the chronicle of this liberation, just like the children's book which he translated, The Little Black fish. The story of a little female fish who chooses the freedom of the sea over the quiet of the little river. As the hero of *Arusi* says, talking about the woman he loves:

Juu ya uso huu shuwari
Zimetanda na kuenea,
Hasa alfajiri
Uso unajuwasha
Kwa uzuri
Na bashasha
Hasa wekundu
Juu yake unapojipitia

Hapo ndipo
Vitu hivi
Kope na nyewele za dukani,
Hutiwa huzuni na haiba inayoingia,

Na haiba
Huwa midomoni
Iliyobenuka
Katika kicheko
Nisichokisikia,
Nina hofu,
Mwenzangu uneniruka
Mimi na haya mazingira pia.

Na umejifikia mwenyewe
Katika ukimya
Ambao ni yako nafsia . (Arusi, 1980:19)

Calm spread across her face
Especially early in the morning her face lights up
With beauty, with happiness
Especially when she blushes

That's when false eye lashes and a wig
Have a sad effect and beauty takes its place!

Beauty is on her lips fringed with laughter
I cannot hear.

I fear my love has gone away
From me and from our world
And that all by itself
it has reached the silence
Which is its true being

Post Script

I returned to Dar es Salaam in April 1997 and met Ebrahim Hussein several times. I showed him my translations, and gave him a copy of the French and Italian editions of his poem on the Berlin Wall. We went for many walks and during one of these I took the photographs for this volume. Ebrahim was glad to see his poem on Berlin in print. He was often in a cheerful mood as we rediscovered meeting places of the Dar of the sixties: Palm Beach terrace, for example. The waiters recognised him and that made him nostalgic. He still works for Oxford University Press, reading manuscripts and translating. He gave me two new poems. I wanted to go to Kilwa with him, but he was not interested in going there again. He still does not want to leave the country for fear of problems at the border. And yet there is a new president, several political parties, a laid-back and peaceful atmosphere and his fears do not really seem to be justified.

I was not able to go to Kilwa. The road was cut off by rain. I took the boat to Mtwara. I sailed past the Kilwa coast, I saw Mikindani, from where the Kilwa caravans had started out for the Great Lakes and from where Livingstone had set out on his last voyage. In Vasco de Gama's time Kilwa was a big city, celebrated by Camoens in the Lusiads. Today it is a port which is not easily accessible, a sleepy town. For how long? Recently, oil was discovered there. We had known all along - for a long time - that the Persian Gulf was not far away!

Arusha, 1 May 1997

Bibliography of the works of Ebrahim Hussein (1943 -)

Hussein, E.
- 1969 *Kinjeketile*, Dar es Salaam/Nairobi, Oxford University Press, p49.
- 1970 *Michezo ya Kuigiza* (Wakati Ukuta, Alikiona), Dar es Salaam:East African Publishing House, p64.
- 1970 *Kinjeketile* (translated from Kiswahili into English by the author), Dar es Salaam:Oxford University Press, pp53.
- 1970 *An Annotated Bibliography of Swahili Theatre*, Mulika, 39, pp49-60
- 1971 *Mashetani*, Dar es Salaam:Oxford University Press, pp57
- 1971 *Ufundi wa M.S. Abdulla*, in F. Topan (ed.), 1971, Oxford University Press, pp.21-26.
- 1975 *On the Development of Theatre in East Africa*, Doctoral thesis, Humboldt University, pp180 & 42.
- 1976 *Jogoo Kijijini, Ngao ya Jadi*, Dar es Salaam:Oxford University Press, p57.
- 1977 'Tale-Telling as a Performing Art' in *Theatre and Social Reality*, edited by J. Fiebach, International Theatre Institute, Berlin, pp50-59.
- 1978 'Ngugi, Ugumu wa ukweli anausema', *Zinduko* No. 3, p36.
- 1980 *Arusi*, Dar es Salaam:Oxford University Press, p50.
- 1981 *Samaki Mdogo Mweusi*, Translated by Ebrahim Hussein, with an introduction (translated from the English version of the Persian text), Dar es Salaam: Tanzania Publishing House, p45.
- 1986 *Usanifu wa Kiswahili na Ushairi Tanzania: Uteuzi wa Maneno*, Lecture given on Radio Tanzania, on the occasion of programmes marking the thirty-fifth anniversary, p11.
- 1988 *Kwenye Ukingo wa Thim*, Nairobi, Oxford University Press, pp39. (previously unpublished translation: At the edge of the Thim, by Kimani Njogu, Nairobi, 1996)
- 1988 Previously unpublished *Conference on Ngugi*, University of Nairobi, p10.
- 1991 *Comment Crire pour le Théatre en Suivant Aristotle?*

(French translation by Kasoro Tumbwe of: *Hatua Mbalimbali za Kubuni na Kutunga Tamthilya Kufuatana ya Misingi ya ki-Aristotle, an excerpt from Fasihi: Makala ya Semina ya Kimataifa ya Waandishi wa Kiswahili*, TUKI: Dar es Salaam, 1983, pp194-202), Nairobi, Travaux et documents du CREDU, p12 reprinted in Alternatives Chéatrales, Brussels, 1995.

1991 Previously unpublished *Introduction to the French Translation of Arusi* (the marriage), CREDU, p3.

1996 'Ukuta wa Berlin' poem in A. Ricard, *E. Hussein, Poeta Tra Mare e Muri, Africa e Mediteraneo*, p45.

1997 'Ukuta wa Berlin' poem in A. Ricard, *Rencontre avec un poète, Traverses de l'Afrique, Cahiers du Centre regional des lettres d'Aquitaine*, p98.

Bibliography

Abdulaziz, M. 1979, *Muyaka: 19th Century Swahili Popular Poetry*, Nairobi: Kenya Literature Bureau.

Alloula, A. 1995, *Les Généreux*, Arles: Actes Sud.

Arens, W. 1975, 'The Waswahili: The Social History of an Ethnic Group' in *Africa*, XLV, 4, pp. 426-328.

Badian, S. 1962, *La Mort de Chaka*, Paris: Présence Africaine.

Balisidya, M. 1972, 'Wakati Ukuta' in *Mulika*, No. 5, pp. 12-17.

—, 1975. *Shida*, Nairobi: Foundation Books.

Batibo, H. & Martin, D. 1989, *Tanzanie, l'Ujamaa Face aux Réalités*, Paris: Editions Recherches sur les Civilisations.

Behrangi, S. 1968, *Mahi e Siyah e Kutchulu* (The Little Black Fish), Téhéran, 1968.

—, 1976 *The Little Black Fish and other Modern Persian Short Stories*, translated from the Persian by M. and E. Hooglund, Washington.

—, 1997, *Il Piccolo Pesce Nero*, unpublished (Italian translation by Natalia Tornecello) Naples: Istituto Universitario Orientale.

—, 1997, *Le Petit Poisson Noir*, French translation, Caen: Le Chardon Bleu.

Bertoncini, E. 1985, *Profilo Della Letteratura Swahili*, Naples: Istituto Universitario Orientale.

—, 1989, *Outline of Swahili Literature*, Leiden: E.J. Brill, p.341.

Borges, J. L. 1962, *La Busca de Averroes* in *El Aleph*, Buenos Aires: Emecé.

Brecht, B. 1978, *Brecht on Theatre*, (edited and translated by J. Willet) London: Methuen.

Camoens L. 1572, *Les Lusiades*, (translated into French and annotated by R. Bismuth) Paris: Robert Laffont (1996) (English translation by Landegwhite Perjuin).

Casalis, E. 1841, *Etudes sur la Langue Séchuana*, Paris.

Césaire, A. 1956, *Cahier d'un Retour au Pays Natal*, Paris: Présence Africaine.

—, 1963, *La Tragédie du Roi Christophe*, Paris: Présence Africaine.

—, 1966, *Une Saison au Congo*, Paris: Le Seuil.

Chittick, N. 1974, *Kilwa: An Islamic Trading City on the East African Coast*, Nairobi: British Institute in Eastern Africa, 2 Vols.

Cliffe, L. et al. 1975, 'Postscript to Mbambara 1972' in *Rural Cooperation in Tanzania*, Dar es Salaam: Tanzania Publishing House, pp. 392-395.

Cliffe, L. & Saul, J. 1972, *Socialism in Tanzania, Vol 1 Politics*, Nairobi: East African Publishing House.

Cohen, D. W. & Athieno Odhiambo, E. S. 1992, *Burying SM: The Politics of Knowledge and the Sociology of Power in Africa*, Portsmouth: Heinemann/James Currey, p.159.

Cole-Beuchat, P. D. 1957, 'Riddles in Bantu' in *African Studies*, 16, 3.

Conteh-Morgan, J. 1994, *Theatre and Drama in Francophone Africa*, Cambridge: Cambridge University Press

Constantin, F. 1983, *Les Communautés Musulmanes d'AfriqueOrientale*, Pau, Crepao.

Constantin, F. 1988, *Condition Swahili et Indentité Politique; Commentaires sur L'éternelle Genèse D'une Non-Ethnicité, in Les Ethnies ont une Histoire*, edited by J.P. Chrétien and G. Prunier, Paris: Karthala, pp337-355.

Copans, J. 1988, (textes recueillis par), *Conférence internationale sur la Déclaration d'Arusha, Travaux et documents du CREDU*, No. 3, p.114.

Darnton, R. 1992, *Dernière Danse sur le Mur, Berlin: 1989-1990*, (translated from American) Paris: Odile Jacob, 282 p.

Dumont, L. 1985, *Essais sur l'individualisme*, Paris: Le Seuil.

Faik-Nzuji, C. 1976, *Devinettes Tonales, Tusumwinu*, Paris: Selaf.

Fiebach, J. 1975, 'On the Social Fiction of Modern African Theatre and Brecht' in *Umma*, 5, 2, pp. 159-171.

—, 1993, *From well made drama to oral performances in Ebrahim Hussein's theatre work-politial significations of literary forms*, Paper presented at the Congress of African Studies Association, New Orleans, 1993.

—, 1997, Ebrahim Hussein's Dramaturgy: A Swahili Multiculturalist's Journey in Drama and Theatre Research in African Literature 1997, 28, 4, pp.19-37.

Fo, D. 1990, *Le Gai Savoir de l'Acteur*, (translated from Italian with drawings by the author) Paris: L'Arche, p.319.

Freeman-Granville, G. S. P. 1965 *The French at Kilwa Island*, Oxford: Clarendon Press.

—, 1988, *Shii Rulers at Kilwa*, London: Variorum Reprints.

Gilsenan, M. 1973, *Saint and Sufi in Modern Egypt*, Oxford University Press.

—, 1982, *Recognizing Islam*, London: Croom Helm.

Grunebaum, G. 1967, Literature in the Context of Islamic Civilization, Oriens: Leiden, vol 20, pp.1-14.

Eastman, C. M. 1971, 'Who are the Waswahili?' in *Africa*, XLI, 3, pp. 228-236.

Harries, L. 1964, 'The Arabs and Swahili Culture' in *Africa*, XXXIV, 3, pp. 224-229.

Hartmann, J., 1987, 'Le Capital Prive en Tanzanie, 1962-1982' in *Politique Africaine*, 26, pp. 73-90.

Hazoumé, P. 1938, *Le pacte de Sang au Dahomey*, Paris:Institut d'ethnologie.

Hino, S. 1968, *The Occupational Differentiation of an African town (Ujiji)*, Kyoto University African Studies, II, pp. 51-74.

Ikambili, H. 1992, *Mwongozo wa Mashetani*, Nairobi: Evans Brothers.

Jeyifo, B. 1985, *The Truthful Lie: Essays in a Sociology of African Drama*, London: New Beacon Books.

Jolles, A. 1972, *Formes Simples*, Paris:Le Seuil.

Kezilahabi, E. 1978, *Utenzi wa Ukombozi wa Zanzibar*, Mulika, 14, pp. 45-51,Unversity of Dar es Salaam.

—, 1979, *Gamba la Nyoka,* Arusha: East African Publications Limited.

—, 1987, *Sofferenza*, translated from Kiswahili *(Kichomi)* by E. Bertoncini, Naples: Plural, p.100.

Khatib, M. 1992, *Taarab Zanzibar,* Dar es Salaam: Tanzania Publishing House.

Kiango, S. D. 1975, *Kitabu Nilichosoma (Makala ya Redio),* Tuki: University of Dar es Salaam, p.76.

Kingei, G. 1987, *Usanifu wa Lugha Katika Uandishi wa Ebrahim Hussein*, Mulika, 1987, 19, pp. 19-35, University of Dar es Salaam.

—, 1987, *Mwongozo wa Mashetani*, Nairobi: Heinemann.

Kitzao, J. 1977, '*Washusika wa Kinjeketile*' in F. Topan (ed.) *Vol 2, Uchambuzi wa Maandishi ya ́ Kiswahili*, Dar es Salaam: Oxford University Press. pp. 22-42.

Knappert, J. 1972, (ed.) *An Anthology of Swahili Love Poetry*, Berkeley/Los Angeles: University of California Press.

Lefort, C. 1976, *Un Homme en Trop, Réflexions sur "l'Archipel du Goulag"* Paris:Le Seuil.

—, 1994, *Lettre au Journal Le Monde à Propos de Salman Rushdie.*

Lihamba, A. 1985, *Politics and Theatre in Tanzania after the Arusha Declaration*, Ph.D., University of Leeds.

Lofchie, M. 1965, *Zanzibar, Background to a Revolution*, Princeton University Press.

Loire, G. 1993, *Gens de Mer à Dar es Salaam*, Paris: Karthala, p.230.

Mazrui, A. 1995, 'Why is our Literature so Stubbornly European?' in *The Sunday Nation*, Nairobi, 20 August.

Martin, D. 1988, *Tanzanie: l'Invention d'une Culture Politique*, Paris: Karthala/Presses de la Fondation Nationale des Sciences Politiques, p.318.

Mcha, Y. 1977, *Wakati ukuta: Mgongano wa Tamaduni*, in F. Topan, (ed.), pp. 12-21.

Médard, J. F. 1988, 'La Veuve, le Clan et la Justice: un Enterrement au Kenya', *Politique Africaine* 29, pp. 109-114.

Mertens, G. 1992, (ed.) *Dictionnaire Français-Kiswahili*, Nairobi: Credu.

Meschonnic, H. 1982, *Critique du Rythme, Anthropologie Historique du Langage*, Lagrasse: Verdier.

Miachina, E. N. (sous la direction de), 1987, *Kamusi ya Kiswahili-Kirusi*, Moscow:Editions de la langue russe.

Mizra, S. 1977, 'Mafunzo ya Kinjeketile' in F. Topan (ed.) *Vol 2, Uchambuzi wa Maandishi ya Kiswahili* Dar es Salaam: Oxford University Press, pp. 1-5.

Mlama, P. 1975, *Pambo*, Nairobi: Foundation Books.

Mnyampala, M. 1965, *Diwani ya Mnyampala*, Nairobi: Kenya Literature Bureau.

Muller, H. 1996, *Guerre sans Bataille: Vie Sous Deux Dictatures*, (translated from German) Paris: l'Arche, 214 p.

Mulokozi, M. M. & Sengo, T. S. 1995, *History of Kiswahili Poetry, AD 1000-2000*, Institute of Kiswahili Research, University of Dar es Salaam, p.133.

Mutebi Mukobwa, J. N. 1985, *Maendeleo ya Maudhui Katika Tamthiliya Tano ya Ebrahim Hussein*, Nairobi University, Master's thesis.

Mvungi, T. 1976, *Mashetani na Mwamko wa Siasa*, Mulika, 13, Unversity of Dar es Salaam. pp. 16-20.

Naipaul, S. 1978, *North of South, An African Journey*, London: André Deutsch.

Ngugi wa Thiong'o 1970, *This Time Tomorrow*, Nairobi: East African Literature Bureau.

Ngugi wa Thiong'o & Mugo, M. 1976, *The Trial of Deadan Kimathi*, London: Heinemann.

Nimtz, A. H. Jr. 1980, *Islam and Politics in East Africa, The Sufi Orders in Tanzania*, Minneapolis: University of Minnesota Press.

Ohly, R. 1978, 'Mashetani Replayed' in *Kiswahili* 48, 1, University of Dar es Salaam, pp. 105-108.

Pachet, P. 1993, *Un à Un, de l'Individualisme en Lit*erature (Michaux, Naipaul, Rushdie), Paris: Le Seuil.

p'Bitek, O. 1969, *The Song of Lawino*, Nairobi: Heinemann Educational.

Philipson, R. 1989, *Drama and National Culture: a Marxist study of Ebrahim Hussein*, Ph.D, University of Wisconsin.

Porée, M. & Massery, A. 1996, *Salman Rushdie*, Paris: Le Seuil.

Ricard, A. 1966, *L'image de la Littérature Occidentale dans la Revue Soviétique Novy Mir, Mémoie de DES dissertation*, Bordeaux University.

— 1992 'Ebrahim's Predicament' in *Research in African Literatures*, 23, 1, pp. 175-178. (cf A.A. Mazrui's letter and A.R.'s answer in the following issue)

—, 1995, Identité et Pouvoir dans l'oeuvre d'Ebrahim Hussein *Bayreuth, Actes du colloque sur l'identite en Afrique.*

—, 1995, *Littératures d'Afrique Noire: des Langues aux Livres*, Paris: CNRS/Karthala.

—, 1997, (ed.) *Traversées de l'Afrique*, Cahiers du Centre regional des lettres d'Aquitaine, 2.

Robert, S. 1967, *Wasifu Wa Siti Binti Saad*, Nelson East Africa.

Roy, O. 1997, *La Nouvelle Asie Centrale*, Paris: Le Seuil.

Ruganda, J. 1972, *The Burdens*, Nairobi: Oxford University Press.

—, 1980, *The Floods*, Nairobi: Heinemann.

—, 1986, *Echoes of Silence*, Nairobi: Heinemann.

Rugyendo, M. 1977, 'The Contest' in *The Barbed Wire and Other Plays*, London: Heinemann.

Rushdie, S. 1991, *Patries Imaginaires*, London: Granta (French translation, 1993).

Sacleux, C. 1939, *Dictionnaire Swahili-Français*, Paris: Institut d'Ethnologie.

Sartre, J. P. 1952, *Saint Genet, Comédien et Martyr*, Paris: Gallimard.

Scarcia, G. 1995, 'Di Qualche Vecchio Shirazi: Parentele O Affinita Sommerse, Parentele O.Affinita Presunte', in *L'Arco di Fango Che Rubo la Luce Alle Stelle, Studi In Onore di Eugenio Guldieri*, Arte et Moneta:Lugano, pp. 303-315.

Sengo, T. S. and Kiango, S. D. 1975, *Ndimi zetu: Uchambuzi wa Maandishi ya Kiswahili*, Dar es Salaam/Nairobi: Foundation Books.

Sengo, T.S. 1976, *Ebrahim Hussein, Mwandishi wa Michezo ya Kuigiza*, TUKI: University of Dar es Salaam,p.35.

—, 1977, 'Alikiona: Uovu tu au Unyama' in F. Topan (ed.) Vol 2, *Uchambuzi wa Maandishi ya Kiswahili*, Dar es Salaam: Oxford University Press. pp. 6-11.

Shakespeare, W. 1964, *Juliasi Kaizari* (Julius Ceasar), translated by J. Nyerere, Dar es Salaam: Oxford University Press.

—, 1969, *Mabepari Wa Venisi* (The Merchant of Venice), translated by J. Nyerere, Dar es Salaam: Oxford University Press.

Steere, E. 1870, *Swahili Tales as told by Natives of Zanzibar*, London

Soyinka, W. 1963, *The Lion and the Jewel*, Oxford University Press.

—, 1965, *A Dance of the Forests*, Oxford University Press.

—, 1967, *Kongi's Harvest*, Oxford University Press.

—, 1975, *Death and the King's Horseman*, Oxford University Press.

Syambo, B. 1988, *Mwongozo wa Kinjeketile,* Nairobi: Heinemann.

Todorov, T. 1984, *Critique de la Critique, un Roman d'Apprentissage*, Paris: Le Seuil.

—, 1989, *Nous et les autres, la réflexion francáise sur la diversité humaine,* Paris: Le Seuil.

Topan, F. 1971, (ed.) Vol 1, *Uchambuzi wa maandishi ya Kiswahili,* Dar.es Salaam: Oxford University Press.

—, 1977, (ed.) Vol 2, *Uchambuzi wa Maandishi ya Kiswahili,* Dar es Salaam: Oxford University Press.

Topp Fargion, J. 1997, *A Zanzibar, Le Taarab des Gens Sans Nom.* Autrepart *Les Arts de la rue dans les Sociétés du Sud,* Cahier des Sciences Humaines de l'Orstom, Nouvelle séries, edited by Michel Agier and Alain Ricard, pp. 59-70.

Traoré, B. 1958, *Le Théâtre Négro-Africain et ses Fonctions Sociales,* Paris: Présence africaine.

Valéry, P. 1960, *Oeuvres,* Paris: La Pléiade.

Werterlund, D. 1980, *Ujamaa na Dini, A study of some aspects of Society and Religion in Tanzania,* 1961-1977, Stockhom: Almqvist and Wiksell.

Yourcenar, M. 1980, *Les Yeux Ouverts, Entretiens Avec Mathieu Galey,* Paris: Le Centurion.

www.ingramcontent.com/pod-product-compliance
Lightning Source LLC
Chambersburg PA
CBHW070945230426
43666CB00011B/2564